Tea Cozies

Tea Cozies

GUILD OF MASTER
CRAFTSMAN PUBLICATIONS

First published 2007 by
Guild of Master Craftsman Publications Ltd
Castle Place, 166 High Street,
Lewes, East Sussex BN7 1XU

Reprinted 2008 (twice)

ISBN: 978-1-86108-500-9

Charts and pattern checking by Carol Chambers
Knitting and crochet illustrations by Simon Rodway

Managing Editor: Gerrie Purcell
Production Manager: Jim Bulley
Editor: Virginia Brehaut
Managing Art Editor: Gilda Pacitti
Design & Photography: Rebecca Mothersole

Set in Gill Sans and Ribbon

Colour origination by Alta Image
Printed and bound in Singapore by Kyodo Printing Co. Ltd.

Why we love tea cozies

An invitation to afternoon tea is the perfect excuse to catch up with a friend and swap life stories. That one simple act of putting on the kettle is such a powerful gesture of friendship that you should never turn it down lightly. How many times has a pot of tea been the excuse to relax for half an hour, plan a wedding, talk babies, ask for advice on relationships and children or plot a great birthday surprise?

Afternoon tea can feature any combination of finger biscuits, dainty sandwiches, scones, jam and cakes. But the one thing you cannot do without is the tea, in a decent teapot, taking centre stage in the ceremony.

But what's this? A naked teapot will never do! Like any leading actor, the teapot deserves the finest textiles the costume department can muster. At *Knitting* magazine we have now held two competitions, inviting readers to design and make tea cozies. As the designs came in, we unwrapped packages with delight, realizing that our readers were as hooked on tea as we are!

Just as tea flows freely in Britain, so did the creativity of knitters. The designs were so good that we just had to turn them into this book. We hope that you will love knitting them, adapting the colours to suit your style. Without further ado, we present this little book as our homage to tea.

Kate Taylor
Editor
Knitting

Contents

Betty Lumley has designed this tea cozy in a colour palette of soft, muted tones. With its simple construction and striking look, it could be knitted in an endless variety of colour combinations and still look like a work of art.

Modern Art

Materials

- Aran or similar yarn (approx 164m/180yd per 100g ball)
- 1 x 100g ball in Natural (A)
- DK oddments (at least 4m long) in Red (B), Pink (C), White (D), Blue (E), Olive (F) and Tan (G) for flowers
- A pair of 4mm (US6, UK8) needles
- Crochet hook 4mm (USD, UK8)

Special techniques

Double crochet – see page 150

Cozy sides – make 2

Using 4mm needles cast on 33 sts.
Work in garter st until work measures
9in (23cm). Cast off.

Gusset

Using 4mm needles cast on 5 sts and
work in garter st until work measures
21½in (55cm). Cast off.

Make basic cozy by matching gusset edge
to cast on edge of one side. Join with a
row of double crochet continuing across
the top and down the cast off edge.
Attach second side and finish with a row
of double crochet round the bottom
edge of the completed cozy.

Flowers

Using 4mm needles and one of the
contrasting colours cast on 43 sts.
1st row: (K1 cast off next 5 sts) rep to
last st, k1. (8 sts).
2nd row: K2 sts into each st (16 sts).
3rd row: Purl.
4th row: Knit.
5th row: P2tog to the end (8 sts).
Thread yarn through sts and sew into
flower shape.
Make as many flowers as you need to
decorate the cozy.

Place flowers as indicated in diagram.

Flower placement

Sarah Keen's simple but sophisticated design would suit
the young professional tea-lover with minimalist tastes
but who always has time for a tea break in their hectic lifestyle.

Contemporary Cool

Materials

- RYC Cashsoft Aran (87m/95yd per 50g ball)
- 1 × 50g ball in Charcoal (A)
- 3 × 50g balls in Blue (B)
- 1 × 50g ball in Cream (C)
  (These amounts include the tea pot stand)
- A pair of 4.5mm (US7, UK7) needles

Special techniques

Intarsia – see page 149

Tension

19 sts × 25 rows measure 4in (10cm) square over st st using 4.5mm needles.

First half

Cast on 49 sts in A and work 6 rows garter st. Break off A and join in B. Using B, begin with a knit row, work st st for 4 rows, knitting the first 2 and last 2 sts on every purl row. Join on the second ball of B and also C and work in patt twisting yarn when changing colours.

Row 1: K22 B, k5C, k22B (second ball).

Row 2: B, k2, p20, p5C, p20 B, k2 (first ball).

Rows 3 & 5: As row 1.

Rows 4 & 6: As row 2.

Row 7: Knit in B (first ball).

Row 8: First ball of B K2, purl to last 2 sts, k2.

Repeat rows 1–8 twice more.

Continue with first ball of B and work 2 rows st st, knitting the first 2 and last 2 sts on purl row.

Begin decreasing

Dec row: K10, (k2tog) twice, k21, (k2tog) twice, k10 (45 sts).

Next row: K2, purl to last 2 sts, k2.

Dec row: K9, (k2tog) twice, k19,(k2tog) twice, k9 (41sts).

Next row: K2, purl to last 2 sts, k2.

Shape top

Dec row: K8, (k2tog) twice, k17, (k2tog) twice, k8 (37 sts).

Next and next 6 foll alt rows: Purl

Dec row: K7, (k2 tog) twice, k15, (k2tog) twice, k7 (33 sts).

Dec row: K6, (k2 tog) twice, k13, (k2tog) twice, k6 (29 sts).

Dec row: K5, (k2 tog) twice, k11, (k2tog) twice, k5 (25 sts).

Dec row: K4, (k2 tog) twice, k9, (k2tog) twice, k4 (21 sts).

Dec row: K3, (k2 tog) twice, k7, (k2tog) twice, k3 (17 sts).

Dec row: K2, (k2 tog) twice, k5, (k2tog) twice, k2 (13sts).

Dec row: k1, (k2 tog) twice, k3, (k2tog) twice, k1 (9 sts).

Break yarn and set aside.

Second half

Work as for first half, do not break yarn.

Join pieces

With wrong sides of work facing, purl across sts of second half and then with the same yarn continue purling across sts of first half (18 sts).

Dec row: (K2tog) to end (9 sts).

Beg with a purl row, work 6 rows st st, ending on a knit row.

Cast off k-wise.

Lining – make 2 pieces

Using A cast on 47 sts and work 6 rows garter st. Break off A and join on B Using B and beg with a knit row, st st 30 rows, knitting the first 2 and last 2 sts on every purl row.

Begin decreasing

Dec row: K10, (k2tog) twice, k19, (k2tog) twice, k10 (43 sts).

Next row & foll alt row: K2, purl to last 2 sts, k2.

Dec row: K9, (k2tog) twice, k17, (k2tog) twice, k9 (39 sts).

Shape top

Dec row: K8, (k2tog) twice, k15, (k2tog) twice, k8 (35 sts).

Next and next 6 foll alt rows: Purl.

Dec row: K7, (k2tog) twice, k13, (k2tog) twice, k7 (31 sts).

Dec row: K6, (k2tog) twice, k11, (k2tog) twice, k6 (27 sts).

Dec row: K5, (k2tog) twice, k9, (k2tog) twice, k5 (23 sts).

Dec row: K4, (k2tog) twice, k7, (k2tog) twice, k4 (19 sts).

Dec row: K3, (k2tog) twice, k5, (k2tog) twice, k3 (15 sts).

Dec row: K1, (k2tog) twice, k1, (k2tog) twice, k1, 7 sts.
Thread yarn through rem sts, pull tight and secure.

Making up
Tea cozy
Join row ends of tea cozy, leaving g-st edges open. Join row ends of garter st band at lower edge.

Lining
Join row ends as for tea cozy, then with wrong sides together, place lining inside tea cozy. Slip st g-st row ends at both openings and then join cast on sts at lower edge, all the way round.

Tea pot stand
Using 4.5mm needles and A, cast on 112 sts.
Dec row: K12, (k2tog) twice, *k24, (k2tog) twice**, rep from * to ** twice, k12 (104 sts).
Next and next 2 foll alt rows: Knit.
Dec row: K11, (k2tog) twice, *k22, (k2tog) twice**, rep from * to ** twice, k11 (96 sts).

Dec row: K10, (k2tog) twice, *k20, (k2tog) twice**, rep from * to ** twice, k10 (88 sts).
Break off A and continue in B.
Dec row: K9, (k2tog) twice, *k18, (k2tog) twice**, rep from * to ** twice, k9 (80 sts).
Next and next 8 foll alt rows: Knit.
Dec row: K8, (k2tog) twice, *k16, (k2tog) twice**, rep from * to ** twice, k8 (72 sts).
Dec row: K7, (k2tog) twice, *k14, (k2tog) twice**, rep from * to ** twice, k7 (64 sts).
Dec row: K6, (k2tog) twice, *k12, (k2tog) twice**, rep from * to ** twice, k6 (56 sts).
Dec row: K5, (k2tog) twice, *k10, (k2tog) twice**, rep from * to ** twice, k5 (48 sts).
Dec row: K4, (k2tog) twice, *k8, (k2tog) twice**, rep from * to ** twice, k4 (40 sts).
Dec row: K3, (k2tog) twice, *k6, (k2tog) twice**, rep from * to ** twice, k3 (32 sts).
Dec row: K2, (k2tog) twice, *k4, (k2tog) twice**, rep from * to ** twice, k2 (24 sts).
Dec row: k1, (k2tog) twice, *k2, (k2tog) twice**, rep from * to ** twice, k1 (16 sts).
Dec row: (k2tog) to end (8 sts).
Thread yarn through remaining sts, pull tight and secure.

Making up
Join row ends.

This fun and quirky cozy knitted by Rosemary Harper will bring a ray of sunshine and warmth to even the greyest winter's day with its vibrantly coloured sunflower motif.

Sunny Delight

Materials

- Patons Washed Haze Aran (approx 92m/100yd per 50g ball)
- 2 × 50g balls in Faded Green (A)
- Patons DK Fab (approx 274m/299yd per 100g ball)
- 1 × 100g ball in each of Yellow (B) and Dark Brown (C)
- 24 wooden beads ³⁄₁₆in (5mm)
- Pair 4.5mm (US7, UK7) needles
- Crochet hook 4mm (USD, UK8)

Tension

18 sts and 24 rows to 4in (10cm).

Special techniques

Double crochet – see page 150

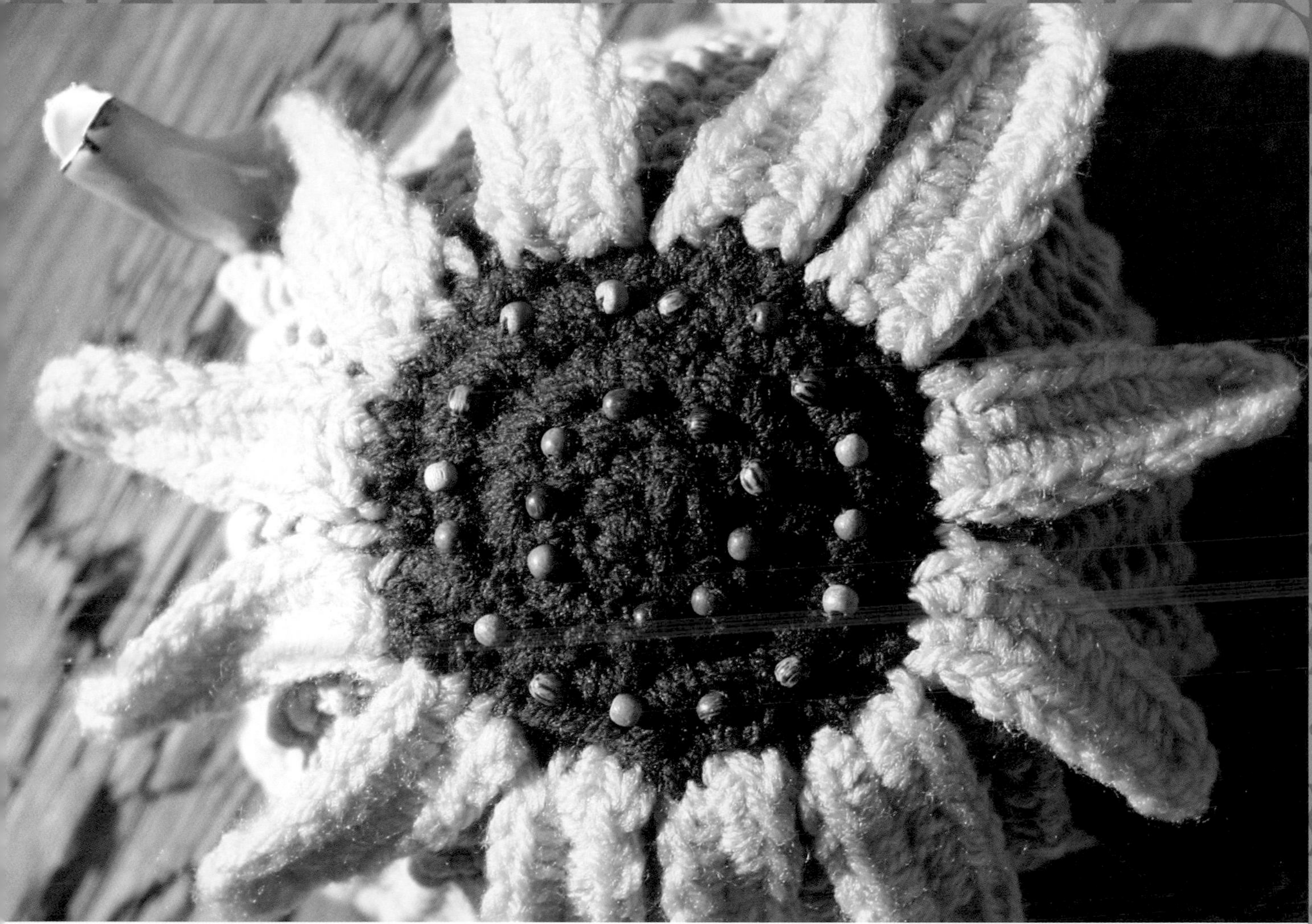

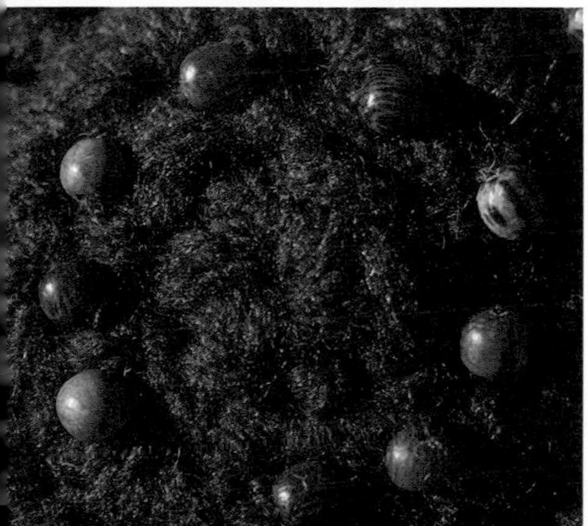

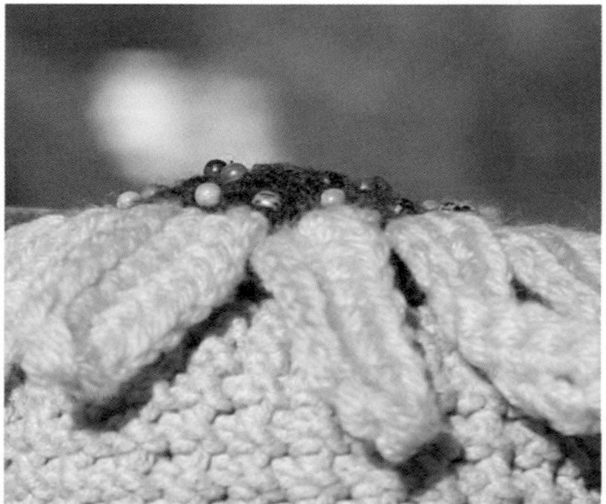

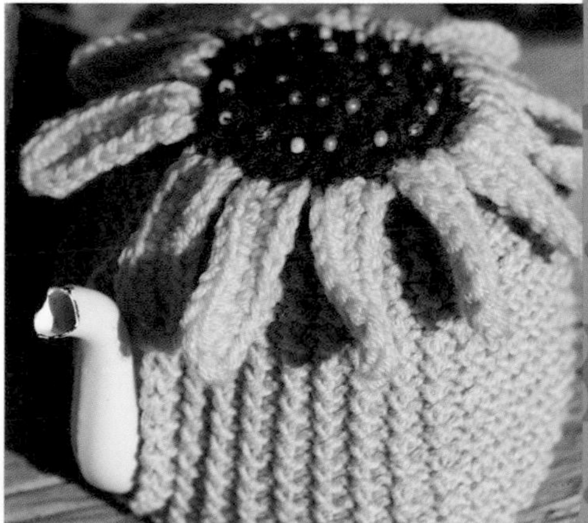

Main piece – make 2

Using A cast on 43 sts.

1st row: P1, k1 tbl, rep from* ending on p1, k1 tbl.

2nd row: Knit.

Work these two rows for 30 rows (adjustable) ending on a knit row. Leave sts on holder and work second side. With RS facing, knit across all sts from both sides.

Knit 1 row.

K2tog along next row (43 sts).

Next row: Knit.

Next row: K2tog 21 times, k1 (22 sts).

Next row: K2tog 11 times.

Next row: Knit.

Next row: K2tog 5 times, k1.

Next row: Knit.

Cut yarn and thread through sts, pull tight and stitch seams leaving appropriate openings for spout and handle.

Petals – make 12

Using crochet hook and 2 strands of B, make 12 chain. Turn and dc into 2nd ch from hook, dc into each foundation chain, 9dc. Work 2 more dc into last ch space and dc into each ch on other side of foundation chain. Work 2 more dc into last space and dc into each st to end. Work 2 more dc into last st and dc into each st of previous round. Fasten off.

Sunflower motif

Working with 2 strands of yarn throughout, make ring and work 6dc into ring, sl st into 1st st.

2nd round: Work 1dc into 1st dc, 2dc into next st, 1dc into next st until round worked, sl st into 1st st.

3rd round: Work 2dc into each st, sl st into 1st st.

4th round: As 2nd.

5th round (joining petals): Hold petal with RS facing, right side of sunflower middle, dc through petal and middle – 3dc to each petal. Space petals evenly round middle and sl st to first st. Sew beads into 2 circles on middle of motif and either sew the completed sunflower onto green tea cozy or crochet to top with dc all round middle, underneath petals to top of tea cozy (i.e. where shaping began). Neaten any remaining loose ends.

In fresh lime green and candy pink, this cheerful design by Lucy Norris makes an eye-catching accessory for your teapot. The intarsia teacup pattern adds a jaunty effect to the finished cozy.

Special Brew

Materials
- Rowan Handknit DK (85m/92yd per 50g ball)
- 2 x 50g balls in 309 Celery (A)
- 1 x 50g ball in each of 310 Shell (B), 313 Slick (C) and 303 Sugar (D)
- A pair of 4mm (US6, UK8) needles

Tension
21 sts measure 4in (10cm) square using 4mm needles.

Special techniques
Intarsia – see page 149

Notes
Wind off small balls of A, B and C for working intarsia teacup pattern.

Side one

With 4mm needles and A cast on 98 sts and knit 7 rows (garter st).

Next row: Knit 49 sts, leave rem 49 sts on holder, turn.

Next row: Purl.

Teacup motif: Use intarsia method, work from chart on facing page, positioning design in centre thus:

Teacup row 1: Knit 22 sts A, 8 sts B (first row of chart), using separate ball of A knit to end.

Work the rem 24 rows of motif as set, ending with 3 rows st st ending with a knit row. Transfer sts from holder onto needle, then transfer sts from other needle (with finished motif) onto holder.

Side two

Knit second side as for first side, swapping the 3 colours' roles if desired (eg swap spots' colour with background colour).

Top

Next row: Purl 48 sts, k1 st; transfer sts from holder to needle and from these k1 st, purl rem 48 sts.

Work 6 rows st st.

Next row: K1 st, * k4 st, k2tog, repeat from * to last st, k1 st.

Work 2 rows st st.

Tip

Don't panic if your intarsia work looks a little messy. Weave the ends into the back and then ease any distorted stitches back into place by pressing lightly under a damp cloth.

Next row: P1 st, * p2tog, p3 st, repeat from * to last st, p1 st.

Work 2 rows st st.

Next row: K1 st, * k2 st, k2tog, repeat from * to last st, k1 st.

Work 2 rows st st.

Next row: P1 st, * p2tog, p1 st, repeat from * to last st, p1 st.

Work 2 rows st st.

Next row: K1 st, * k2tog, repeat from * to last st, k1 st.

Next row: *p2tog, rep from * 9 times in all, 9 sts.

Next row: Change to B, k1, *k2tog, rep from * to end, 5 sts.

Next row: k2, k2tog, k1, 4 sts. Break off yarn leaving a good end. Thread yarn through rem 4 sts dropping them off needle. Pull thread up tight and fasten off.

Making up

Sew up side of tea cozy at top and bottom to match other side. Press.

Special Brew Chart *29 sts x 25 rows*

Work in st st. Each square = 1 st and 1 row. Read RS rows from R to L
and WS (purl) rows from L to R.

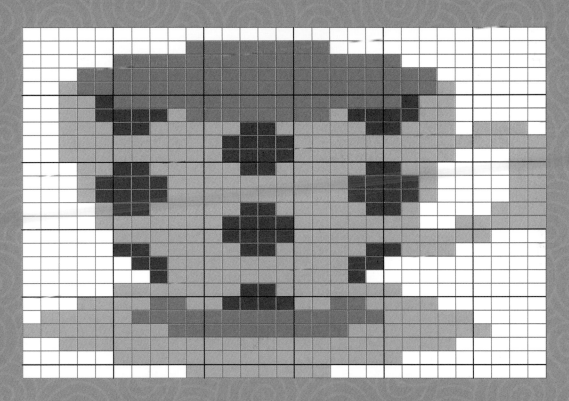

■ A
■ B
■ C
■ D

Classic stripes are guaranteed to harmonize with almost any decor from rustic and homely to modern and sleek. Sarah Keen's design could find a place in every tea-lover's home.

Stripey Sensation

Materials

- RY Cashsoft Aran (87m/95yd per 50g ball)
- 3 × 50g balls in Terracotta (A)
- 1 × 50g ball in each of Ecru (B) and Deep Blue (C)
- 1 pair each of 3.75mm (US5, UK9) and 4.5mm (US7, UK7) knitting needles

Tension

19 sts and 25 rows to 4in (10cm) square.

First half

Using 4.5mm needles, A and the one needle method of casting on such as the continental (long tail) or thumb method, cast on 50 sts and work 6 rows garter st. Join on B and C and work in st st in stripes, carrying yarn loosely up sides of work.

Row 1: B, knit 1 row.
Rows 2–4: C, beg with a purl row st st 3 rows.
Row 5: A, knit 1 row.
Rows 6–8: B, st st 3 rows.
Row 9: C, knit 1 row.
Rows 10–12: A, st st 3 rows.
Rows 1–12 set the pattern and are rep once more.
Next row: B, knit 1 row.
Next row: C, purl 1 row.

Begin decreasing

Dec row: C *(k10, k2tog) rep from * to last 2 sts, k2 (46 sts).
Next row: C, purl 1 row.
Dec row: A *(k9, k2tog) rep from * to last 2 sts, k2 (42 sts).
Next row: B, purl 1 row.
Place a marker on first and last st.

Shape top

Dec row: B *(k8, k2tog) rep from * to last 2 sts, k2 (38 sts).

Next row: B, purl 1 row.
Dec row: C *(k7, k2tog) rep from * to last 2 sts, k2 (34 sts).
Next row: A, purl 1 row.
Dec row: A *(k6, k2tog) rep from * to last 2 sts, k2 (30 sts).
Next row: A, purl 1 row.
Dec row: B *(k5, k2tog) rep from * to last 2 sts, k2 (26 sts).
Next row: C, purl 1 row.
Dec row: C *(k4, k2tog) rep from * to last 2 sts, k2 (22 sts).
Next row: C, purl 1 row.
Dec row: A *(k3, k2tog) rep from * to last 2 sts, k2 (18 sts).
Next row: B, purl 1 row.
Dec row: B *(k2, k2tog) rep from * to last 2 sts, k2 (14 sts).
Next row: B, purl 1 row.
Dec row: C *(k1, k2tog) rep from * to last 2 sts, k2 (10 sts).
Break yarn and set aside.

Second half

Work as for first half but don't break yarn.
Continue in A.
Join pieces
With wrong sides facing, purl across sts of second half, and then with the same yarn continue purling across sts of first half, 20 sts.
Dec row: *(k2tog) rep from * to end (10 sts).
Dec row: P1, *(p2tog, p1) rep from * to end (7 sts).
Inc row: K1, *(m1, k1) rep from * to end (13 sts).
Beg with a purl row, work 4 rows st st, ending on a k row.
Cast off k-wise, loosely.

Lining – make 2 pieces

Begin at lower edge using 4.5mm needles, A and the one-needle method of casting on and cast on 46 sts. Work 6 rows garter st.
Beg with a knit row, st st 30 rows, knitting the first and last st on every purl row.

Begin decreasing

Dec row: *(k9, k2tog) rep from * to last 2 sts, k2 (42 sts).
Next row: K1, purl to last st, k1.
Dec row: *(k8, k2tog) rep from * to last 2 sts, k2 (38 sts).

Next row: K1, purl to last 2 sts, k1. Place a marker on first and last st of last row.

Shape top

Dec row: *(k7, k2tog) rep from * to last 2 sts, k2, 34 sts.

Next row and foll 6 alt rows: purl.

Dec row: *(k6, k2tog) rep from * to last 2 sts, k2 (30 sts).

Dec row: *(k5, k2tog) rep from * to last 2 sts, k2 (26 sts).

Dec row: *(k4, k2tog) rep from * to last 2 sts, k2 (22 sts).

Dec row: *(k3, k2tog) rep from * to last 2 sts, k2 (18 sts).

Dec row: *(k2, k2tog) rep from * to last 2 sts, k2 (14 sts).

Dec row: *(k1, k2tog) rep from * to last 2 sts, k2 (10 sts).

Dec row: *(k2tog) rep from * to end (5 sts). Thread yarn through rem sts, pull tight and secure.

Making up and edging
Tea cozy

With right sides together, place both halves of tea cozy together, matching all edges and join row ends from top to markers by sewing back and forth one st in from edge. Turn right side out.
Work edging for spout and handle
Using 3mm needles and A, with RS facing pick up and knit 58 sts from around each opening between garter st bands.
Cast off k-wise.
Join row ends of garter st bands.

Lining

Join row ends as for tea cozy then with WS together, place lining inside tea cozy. Working from the inside, slip-st lining to tea cozy around both openings for spout and handle. Join cast on sts at lower edge all the way round.

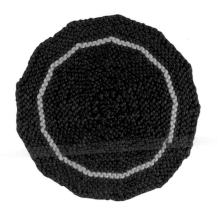

Teapot stand

Teapot stand is worked in garter st. Using A, 4.5mm needles and using the one-needle method of casting on, cast on 104 sts and knit 2 rows.

Dec row: *(k6, k2tog) rep from * to end, 91 sts.

Work 3 rows garter st.
Break off A and join on B.

Dec row: *(k5, k2tog) rep from * to end, 78 sts.

Knit 1 row.
Break off B and join on C.

Work 2 rows garter st.

Dec row: *(k4, k2tog) rep from * to end (65 sts).

Work 3 rows garter st.

Dec row: *(k3, k2tog) rep from * to end (52 sts).

Work 3 rows g-st.

Dec row: *(k2, k2tog) rep from * to end (39 sts).

Work 3 rows garter st.

Dec row: *(k1, k2tog) rep from * to end (26 sts).

Work 3 rows garter st.

Dec row: *(k2tog) rep from * to end (13 sts).

Knit 1 row.
Thread yarn through sts, pull tight and secure.

Making up

Join row ends.

Impress your tea party guests with this quirky cozy by Vicki Walker.
Its bold colour with a twist of eccentricity and funky spirals means
it will always stand out brightly in a crowd.

Pink Twist

Materials

- SWTC Karaoke or DK yarn of your choice
  (100m/109yd per 50g ball)
- 1 × 50g ball in (A)
- Katia Pinta Print (80m/87.5yd per 50g ball)
- 1 × 50g ball in (B)
- 1 yd (0.75m) × 7in (18cm) of lining fabric.
- A pair of 4mm (US6, UK8) needles
- 2 × 4mm (US6, UK8) double-pointed (dp)
  needles (optional)
- 8 × stitch markers

Special abbreviations

sm: slip marker

mt: Make spiral. Join in B. Using dp needle knit next st.
Using this st and second dp needle cast on 19 sts (20 sts),
k2tog 10 times, casting off 9 (spiral) sts as you go (i.e. k2tog,
k2tog, cast off along row – you should end alongside main
fabric). Slip rem st onto LH needle and knit
with A. Break off B.

Sides – make 2

With 4mm needles and B, cast on 40 sts.

Row 1: Purl.

Row 2: Knit.

Join in A and break off B.

Row 3: Using A, knit and at the same time place markers after 5th, 15th, 25th and 35th sts.

Row 4 and then every even numbered row: Purl.

Row 5: Knit to 1st before 1st marker, m1, sm, knit to 1st before 2nd marker, m1, sm, knit to 3rd marker, sm, m1, knit to 4th marker, sm, m1.

Row 7: Knit to 1st before 1st marker, mt, knit to 1st before 2nd marker, mt, knit to 3rd marker, sm, mt, knit to 4th marker, sm, mt, knit to end.

Row 9: As row 5.

Row 11: Knit.

Row 13: As row 5.

Row 15: As row 7 BUT for mt cast on 18 sts and k2tog 9 times.

Row 17: As row 5.

Row 19: Knit.

Row 21: Knit to 1st marker, k2tog, sm, knit to 2nd marker, k2tog, sm, knit to 3rd marker, sm, k2tog, knit to 4th marker, sm, k2tog.

Row 23: As row 7 BUT for mt cast on 16 sts and k2tog 8 times.

Row 25: As row 21.

Row 27: Knit.

Row 29: As row 21.

Row 31: As row 7 BUT for mt cast on 14 sts and k2tog 7 times.

Row 33: As row 21.

Row 35: Knit.

Row 36: Purl.

Leave this side on a spare needle.

Top

When the second side has been completed to row 36, join in B and knit across all sts on 2nd side and 1st side to join the pieces together. Leave markers in place.

Row 38: Knit.

Row 39: Purl.

Join in A.

Row 40: Purl.

Row 41: (RS facing) knit.

Row 42: (P to 2 sts before marker, p2tog, sm, p2tog), rep to end.

Row 43 and then every odd numbered row to row 51: Knit.

Rows 44, 46 and **48:** As row 42.

Row 50: Purl, removing markers as you go.

Row 51: K2tog across row.

Row 52: Purl.

Join in B.

Row 53: As row 51.

Row 54: Knit.

Row 55: P2tog across row.

Row 56: K3tog.

With rem 1 st, mt, casting on 29 sts (30 sts). Fasten off.

Making up

Using tail from top spiral, secure spiral and sew seam together only as far as B goes.

Using A continue to sew seam to approximately 1in (3cm) past the B ridge. On the other side opening, sew seam to approximately 1in (3cm) past the yarn B ridge.

Using B join bottom of each side where B is at the bottom of the cozy.

You should now sew in any remaining loose ends apart from those on the spirals which can be neatly knotted and cut. They will be hidden by the lining.

Lining

Cut 2 rectangles from your lining fabric 12in (30cm) x 7in (18cm) and cut a circle with a diameter of 5in (12cm). With the wrong side of your tea cozy facing outwards, lay one piece of the lining fabric onto one side of the cozy. Turning under ⅜in (1cm) all the way round, stitch the lining directly onto cozy along the bottom edge and up the 2 sides. Repeat for the second side, catching the 2 lining pieces together above the spout and handle holes. Lay the circle on the top of the cozy. Pin it in place and with ⅜in (1cm) turned under stitch around the circle to secure it to the tops of the side lining pieces.

It's not necessary to fit the lining perfectly as any bagginess allows a bit of stretch in the knitting.

You can be bold or mellow with your choice of colours for this cozy by Karen Holdup. Striking contrast or muted tones work equally well to create a stunning effect.

Check Mate

Materials
- Stylecraft Special DK (302m/332yds per 100g ball)
- 1 × 100g ball in each of Bright Pink and Sunshine
- 1 × 50g ball in Fleet
- 3 × 4mm (US6, UK8) needles
- Small amount of toy stuffing

Special techniques
- Double rib – see page 145
- Fair isle – see page 149

Alternative colourway
- British Breeds Blue Face Leicester DK
- 1 × 50g ball in Denim
- 1 × 50g ball in Fleet

Bottom triangles

Cast on 1 st in pink.

Inc 1 k-wise, 2 sts.

In st st starting with a purl row, inc 1
each end every 2nd row to 14 sts and
leave on needle.

Make 8 triangles and leave all on same
needle, facing the same way.

Ribbing

In yellow cast on 122 sts and work in
double rib for 5 rows.

Next row: in rib work 60 sts, cast off 2
sts and work rem 60 sts in rib.

From here on work one 60 st side at a
time to create centre opening.

Work double rib for another 5 rows.

Main body

Hold needle with triangles and needle
with rib parallel, k side facing forward
and open ends of needles together.
Graft rib and triangles together by
knitting through both layers and leaving
1 st between each triangle, in pink. Follow
chart A for each side. With both sides on
the same needle, work straight across all
120 sts following chart B. Leave good
amount of yarn and cut. Thread sewing
needle and pass through sts, take off
needle and pull tight and fasten off. Fold
in half and sew from top end down and
from bottom end up creating spout slit.
'Pin' bottom points of triangles to
bottom rib edge with a couple of sts.
Sew in all loose ends.

Tip

*The strong shapes in this pattern
mean it looks fantastic in contrasted
or muted colourways. Yarn details for
blue version are on page 35*

Top

Make 3 of each colour.

Cast on 1 st. Inc 1 k-wise, 2 sts.

Starting with a purl row, continue in st
st, inc 1 each end every 2nd row until
12 sts.

Starting with a purl row, continue in st st,
dec 1 each end every 2nd row until 1 st
and cast off.

Sew together top edges, alternating
colours to form circle.

Sew in all loose threads.

Sew to centre of top, covering hole.

Bobble

Cast on 12 sts.

Next row: Purl.

Next row: K2, inc in next 3 sts, k2, inc in
next 3 sts, k2.

Starting with a purl row, continue in st st
and work 2 rows.

Next row: *P2, (p2tog)3 times, rep
from * once more, p2 (12 sts).

Next row: K1,(k2tog) 5 times, k1
(7 sts). Thread yarn through rem sts and
pull tight. Fasten off.

Making up

Right sides together, sew sides together
and turn right side out.

Gather by threading yarn through cast
on edge and leave loose.

Stuff firmly and pull gathers tight and
fasten off.

Sew bobble to the centre of the top.

Chart A - left

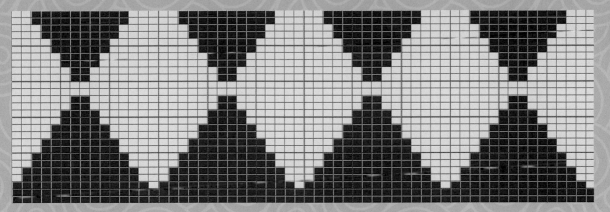

Chart A - right

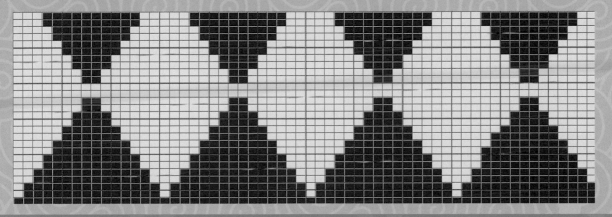

Chart B

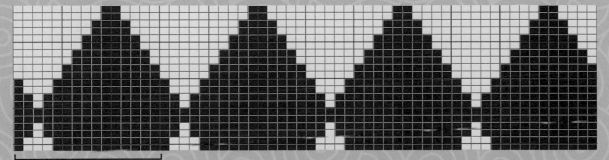

Repeat

Sue Faulkner's design is a wonderful, watery surprise. Enjoy your refreshing cup of tea along with jaunty seahorses bobbing alongside colourful seaweed and anemones.

Seashore Surprise

Materials
- Paton's Diploma Gold (120m/131yd per 50g ball).
- 1 x 50g ball in each of Mermaid (A), Aqua (B), Honey (C), Cyclamen (D), Hollyhock (E), White (F)
- Oddment of Navy.
- A pair of size 3.25mm (US3, UK10) needles
- A pair of size 4mm (US6, UK8) needles
- Crochet hook 3.25mm (US3, UK10)

Tension
22 sts and 30 rows to 4in (10cm) square.

Special techniques
- Double rib – see page 145
- Intarsia – see page 149
- Fair Isle – see page 149
- double crochet – see page 150
- half treble – see page 151
- treble – see page 151

Tea Cozies

Seashore Surprise Chart *22 sts x 26 rows*

Work in st st. Each square = 1 st and 1 row.

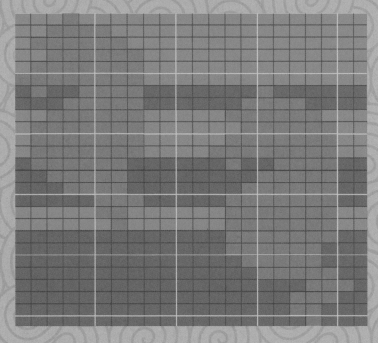

A
B
C

Main pieces – make 2

With colour A and 3.25mm needles cast on 54 sts.

Row 1: (k2, p2) to end k2.

Row 2: (p2, k2) to end p2.

Rep these rows 5 times, inc at each end of the last row (56 sts).

Change to size 4mm needles.

Starting with a knit row, complete the 26 rows of the chart in stocking stitch as follows:

Knit row 1–22 twice then rows 1 to 11 once, k1.

Decrease rows

Row 1: (With colour B k2, with colour A k2, with B k2, with B ssk) 7 times (49 sts).

Row 2: (With colour B p3, with A p2, with B p2) 7 times.

Row 3: With B k to end.

Row 4: With B p to end.

Row 5: (With A k2, with B k3, with B ssk) 7 times (42 sts).

Row 6: (With B p4, with A p2) 7 times.

Row 7: With B k to end.

Row 8: With B p to end.

Row 9: (With colour B k2, with colour A k2, with B ssk) 7 times (35 sts).

Row 10: (With colour B p1, with A p2, with B p2) 7 times.

Row 11: With B (k3, ssk) 7 times (28 sts).

Row 12: With B p to end.

Row 13: (With A k2, with B ssk) 7 times (21 sts).

Row 14: (With B p1, with A p2) 7 times.

Row 15: With B (k1, ssk) 7 times (14 sts).

Row 16: With B p to end.

Row 17: With B ssk 7 times (7 sts). Fasten off.

Press both pieces.

Decoration

With colour D crochet a chain approximately 8in (20cm), leaving a long tail of about 12in (30cm). Leave the final loop on a holder so that you can add more to the chain or take it back.

With a blunt-ended needle take the tail from front to back just above the ribbing; use the tail to sew the chain into place with running stitches, making it wave as shown. Adjust the chain so that it finishes at the gathered stitches at the top but leave both ends of colour D on the wrong side of the work. Repeat this for as many pieces of seaweed as you choose. With the navy blue oddments add 'eyes' to the seahorses with French knots. To create the anemones,

embroider a star of straight stitches with colour F with a blunt-ended needle. Be careful not to pull them too tight. Go over the star with colour E in the same way.

Making up

Sew the two main pieces together as follows. On the spout side sew approximately 2½in (6cm) from the bottom and 4½in (11cm) from the top. On the handle side sew approximately 2in (5cm) from the bottom and 3½in (9cm) from the top.

With colour D and crochet hook and starting from the bottom, do a row of double crochet around the spout, finishing with a slip stitch. Miss one crochet stitch and create a shell in the next by putting one double crochet, one half treble, one treble, one half treble and a double crochet all into the one stitch, miss next crochet stitch and slip stitch into the next. Continue in this way around the spout opening, adjusting the shells at the end if necessary. Complete the shells around the handle in the same way.

Sew a large anemone around the gathered stitches at the top and pull all the long ends of colour D through the gathered stitches onto the right side. Sew them down and cut to fit.

Delicately smocked with pearly beads and silk ribbon, this design by Margaret Kelleher is perfect for a genteel afternoon tea party with fancy cakes and refined company.

Beaded Beauty

Materials

- Lang Baby Cotton Bambini or other 4 ply yarn (155m/169yd per 50g ball)
- 1 x 50g ball in White (A)
- A pair of 3.25mm (US3, UK10) needles
- 1yd (1m) narrow ribbon
- Approx 44–48 large beads (used for bottom trim, see picture)
- Approx 100 small beads (used for main smocking trim, see picture)

Tension

24 sts and 32 rows to 4in (10cm) square.

Special techniques

- Purl 3, knit 1 rib – instructions in pattern
- Smocking – instructions in pattern

Smocked knitting

Knit the basic pattern in the usual way, in this case a 3 purl and 1 knit rib with additional knit stitches to show where ribs will be stitched together. Beads sit on top of each smocking stitch.

Side 1

Using 3.25mm needles and Bambino wool, cast on 69 sts.
Row 1: (RS) k1, (p3, k1) to end.
Row 2: P1 (k3, p1) to end.
Rows 3 & 4: As rows 1 & 2.
Row 5: As row 1.
Row 6: P1, (k1, p3) to last 4 sts, K3, p1.
Row 7: As row 1.
Rows 8 & 9: As rows 1 & 2.
Row 10: P5, (k3, p5) to end.
Rep rows 1–10 until 50 rows have been worked.

Shape top

Row 1: K1, p2, k2tog, (p2, k2tog) to end.
Row 2: K3, p1, (k2, p1) to end.
Row 3: K1, (p1, yf, k2tog) to end.
Row 4: P1, k2 to end.
Row 5: P2 k1 to end.
Row 6–11: As rows 4 & 5, 3 times.
Cast off loosely in pattern.
Side 2, as side 1.

Making up

Press lightly under a dry cloth using a cool iron. Sew pieces together, leaving an opening for spout and handle. Thread ribbon through eyelet row at top and tie in a bow.

To smock tea cozy

At rows 6 and 10 the pattern is set up to facilitate easy smocking.

1. Bring the darning needle up to the front of the work to the left of the rib st. Stitch into the knit st at the left across the front into the knit st at the right.

2. Pull the ribs together by tightening the st.

3. Add beads onto thread and repeat sewing.

4. Smocked fabric becomes heavy, firm and about 25% narrower after it has been stitched so knit an extra-large tension swatch to account for this (if using finer wool, extra stitches, will be needed). Lining optional.

If you enjoy the company of cats, this cozy by Dee Daniell will make sure tea time is always lively with this delightful fluffy friend to share your well-earned break.

Fluffy Friend

Materials

- Fil a Tricoter Yarn
- 1 x 50g ball in each of Black(B), White (W) and Mixed (black/grey/white) (M)
- Any make or colour scheme of this feather-style yarn works as well with this pattern
- A pair of 5mm (US8, UK6) knitting needles
- 19½in (50cm) cotton fabric
- 19½in (50cm) polyester wadding
- Clip or screw-in eyes (for face, from craft shops)
- Embroidery silks (pink and brown for nose and mouth)
- White mohair wool for whiskers
- Strong darning needle

Body

Using B cast on 60 sts and k10 rows.
Using M knit 2 rows.
Using B knit 6 rows.
Rep last 8 rows until work measures 17in (43cm).
Using B knit 4 rows and cast off.

Head

Using M cast on 20 sts and knit 4 rows
Next row: Using B k4 m1 to end, 24 sts.
Next row: Knit.
Next row: K3 m1 to end, 30 sts.
Knit 3 rows.
Next row: Using M k2 m1 to end, 40 sts.
Next row: Knit.
B knit 4 rows.
Next row: B k15, W k10, B k15.
Next row: B k15, W p10, B k15.
Next row: M k15, W k2, m1 to end of W sts, M k15.
Next row: M k15, W purl to end of W sts, M k15.
Next row: B k15, W k3, m1 to end of W sts, B k15.
B k15, W purl to end of W sts, B k15
B k13, W k4, m1 (4 times), k2, B k13
B k11, W purl (30 sts), B k11
With same colours k5, k2tog to end
B knit, W purl, B knit.
K4, k2tog to end using M and W.
M knit, W purl, M knit.
K3, k2tog to end using B and W
B knit, W purl, B knit.
B k11, W k11, B k11.

B k13, W p7, B k13
K2, k2tog to end using B and W
B knit, W purl, B knit.
K3, k2tog to end using M and W
M knit to end.
B k2, k2tog to end.
B knit.
B k1, k2tog to end.
Cast off loosely.

Tail

Using B cast on 20 sts and knit until work measures 6in (12cm).
B dec 1 st at each end of every alt row until work measures 7in (16cm).
W cont to knit and dec as before until 1 st left, cast off.

Ears (knit 2)

Using B cast on 12 sts and knit until work is a small square and cast off.

Making up

Fold squares for ears in half and stitch sides. Stitch up sides of head and stuff with scraps of wadding. Place eyes, attach ears, stitch nose and mouth, and stitch in whiskers. Fold body in half and fold in top corners and overstitch one side leaving other side open for attaching head later.

Cut out lining and padding – lining 4in (10cm) extra to allow 2in (5cm) bottom hem. Pin and tack the padding and lining together, folding lining hem over the padding. Joint top sides and bottom hems with permanent stitching (can be machined). Place inside cat's body and pull to shape before tacking into place. Stitch lining and padding to the body side openings, overstitch side seams.

Stitch up tail and stuff with scraps of wadding. Attach tail at the left side and either stitch to the body or use Velcro strips. Firmly attach head to the right opening, stitching through lining and wadding. Make a loop (optional) to attach for hanging.

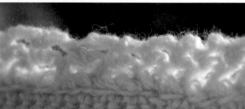

A tea-loving gardener's dream, this design by Anita Ursula-Nycs mixing crochet and embroidered detailing will bring you summery warmth all year round.

Cottage Garden

Materials

- Aran yarn wool/synthetic mix
  (approx 164m/180yd per 100g ball)
- 1 × 100g ball in Cream (A)
- Oddments of chunky yarn in Purple (B)
- Oddments of 4 ply yarn in Blue (C) and Green (D)
- Small oddment of 4 ply metallic yarn
  (E – for butterfly body)
- Oddments of fancy textured yarn
  (for French knot embroidery at base)
- 3.5mm (USE/4, UK9) and 4.5mm (US7, UK7)
  Crochet hooks

Special techniques

- Chain stitch – see page 150
- Double crochet – see page 150

Main body – make 2

Work 2 pieces alike.

Using a 4.5mm hook and A, make 39 ch. Miss 1 ch. Dc in 38 ch (remembering to add one turning ch at beg of each row). Work until piece measures 8in (20cm). Fasten off.

Gusset strip

Using a 4.5mm hook and A, make 16 ch. Miss 1 ch, dc into 15 ch (remembering to add the turning ch at beg).

Work until the strip fits round three sides of the tea cozy. Fasten off.

Flower – make 6

Using 4.5mm hook and B, make 6 chs, join into a circle with a sl st. 1 ch and 7 dc into the ring, sl st to first ch, dc all the way round, ending with a sl st in the first ch and beg each row with 1 ch. Work 1 more row. (Another row can be added, if desired.)

Then work 4 ch, miss 1 dc, dc into next ch, 3 ch, dc into next ch, rep until end. Sl st into base of first st. Fasten off.

Butterfly (small circle) – make 2

Using C and 3.5mm hook, make 6 ch, sl st to form a circle. Work 6 dc into the ring. (Another row of dc can be added, if desired.) Fasten off with a sl st.

Large wing (large oval) – make 2

Using 3.5mm hook and C, work 8 ch, join with a sl st. Work 6 dc, 1 half tr, 1 tr, 8 dc into ring. Fasten off.

Body – make 1

Using E double and 3.5mm hook, work 8 ch. Work 1 or 2 rows of dc. Fasten off. Any finer thread can be used for the body.

Making up

When the 3 main parts have been crocheted, start the placement of the crochet flowers and wool embroidery.

Positioning of crochet flowers

Find the centre on the 2 squares. Attach the first flower. When attaching the first flower, attach it on its reversed side so that a bit of a ridge shows in the centre. Back stitch round the centre of the flower so that it is attached firmly to the background square. Place the other 2 flowers at both sides of the central flower and attach in the same manner. Now embroider the flower stems using D in chain stitch.

Embroider the grass by using straight stitch all along the bottom of the square. Using the fancy yarn, make the French knots, on the grass stalks. Embroider the two leafy stalks and the stalks with the lilac buds in chain stitch and 3-times chain stitch for the buds.

Tip

It can be tricky to keep crocheted edging even. If you are unhappy with the first attempt, simply unravel and start again.

Join the large wing of the butterfly to the small wing using a small overcast stitch. Repeat this twice. Attach the body to the wings by using small back stitches. Attach the butterfly to the grass, near the lilac buds. Do not make another butterfly on the other square piece. The butterfly is only attached to one side of the work.

Gusset strip

Embroider the branch in chain stitch, embroider the buds in chain stitch — treble. Then add the sequins.

Join the gusset strip to the left side of the square using a small back stitch. When this is done using 4.5mm hook work 4ch, 1 dc into both gusset strip and rectangle leaving a 3/8in (1cm) gap. Repeat the process around the 3 sides of the square.

Work another row, starting with 4 chains, 1 double crochet into next chain, to the end. Fasten off.

Attach the other square in the same manner to the gusset strip.

Lining

Make the lining by cutting the lining 3/8in (1cm) bigger than the main three pieces. Fold the lining under for 3/8in (1cm) and attach on the wrong side of the tea cozy by using a small overcast stitch.

Full of character and a unique scruffy charm, this design
by Maud Tabron will suit those without airs and graces –
the down-to-earth tea drinker.

Old Man's Hat

Materials

- Rowan Cork (110m/120yd per 50g ball)
- 2 × 50g balls in 044 Earthy (A – use 2 strands)
- Richard Poppleton's Sierra
- 100g in 643 dull brown (B – lopi style use single thickness)
- Oddments of 4 ply (fingering/sport) yarn (for patches)
- 1 pair each of 3mm (US 2–3, UK11), 6.5mm (US10.5, UK3) and 7.5mm (US11, UK1) needles

Special techniques

- Fair isle – see page 149
- Single rib – see page 145
- Double rib – see page 145

Tension

11.5 sts and 18 rows to 4in (10cm) square
on fronts using 7.5 mm needles.

Linings – make 2

Using 6.5mm needles and B, cast on 31 sts. Work in st st for 12 rows.

Shape top

Row 1: K1, *k2tog, k8; rep from * to end (28 sts).

Rows 2–4: St st.

Row 5: K1, *k2tog, k7, rep from * to end (25 sts).

Rows 6–8: St st.

Row 9: K1, *k2tog, k6, rep from * to end (22 sts).

Rows 10 &12: Purl.

Row 11: K1, *k2tog, k5, rep from * to end (19 sts).

Row 13: K1, *k2tog, k4, rep from * to end (16 sts).

Rows 14–16: St st.

Row 17: K1, *k2tog, k3, rep from * to end (13 sts).

Row 18: Purl.

Row 19: K1, *k2tog, k2; rep from * to end (10 sts).

Row 20: *P1, pP2tog; rep from * to last st, p1 (7 sts).

Row 21: K1, k2tog 3 times (4 sts).

Row 22: P1, (purl into the front and back of the next st) twice, p1 (6 sts).

Row 23: Knit into the front and back of every stitch (12 sts).

Row 24: Purl.

Cast off.

Fronts – make 2

Using 7.5mm and A cast on 31 sts and work in single (k1, p1 rib) for 4 rows. Then work in st st for 10 rows.

You will need to cut off small lengths of yarn to complete the next section.

Place the holes as follows:

Work 7 sts, cast off 5 sts, work 7 sts, cast off 5 sts and work 7 sts.

Work 4 rows only knitting the 3 groups of 7 sts.

Next row: Cast on 4 sts over the 5 cast off (29 sts).

Purl 1 row.

Shaping rows

Row 1: K1, *k2tog, k5; rep from * to end (25 sts).

Rows 2–4: St st.

Row 5: K1, *k2tog, k4, rep from * to end (21 sts).

Rows 6–8: St st.

Row 9: K1, *k2tog, k3; rep from * to end (17 sts).

Row 10: Purl.

Row 11: K1, *k2tog, k2, rep from * to end (13 sts).

Row 12: P1, *p2tog, rep from * to end (7 sts).

Row 13: K1, k2tog 3 times (4 sts).

Row 14: P1, (purl into the front and back of the next st) twice, p1 (6 sts).

Row 15: Knit into the front and back of every st (12 sts).

Row 16: Purl.

Cast off.

Patches

You can use yarn and patterns of your choice for the patches. They just need to be big enough to cover the holes.

Patch 1: *Stripes*

Using 3mm needles and 4 ply yarn cast on 14 sts and work in st st for 16 rows. (Change colour every 2 rows to make a striped pattern using the following colours: mustard, maroon, dark green, rust, olive, cream, turquoise and grey.)

Patch 2: *Double rib using beige*

Using 3mm needles and 4 ply yarn cast on 20 sts and work in double rib (K2, P2) for 16 rows.

Patch 3: *St st using multi-coloured tweed*

Using 3mm needles cast on 14 sts and work in st st for 16 rows.

Patch 4: *Fair isle*

Using 3mm needles cast on 14 sts and work in a Fair isle pattern (see Fair isle chart) for 12 rows. I used maroon (A), green (B) and yellow (C) on a cream (D) background.

Making up

Sew patches 1 and 2 to the inside of one of the fronts and patches 3 and 4 to the inside of the other front covering the holes. Make sure patches face outwards. Turn up the rib at the bottom of the fronts and then with the right sides facing outwards, sew the fronts to the linings. Then sew the two pieces together at the top and the bottom of the sides, leaving holes for the spout and the handle. I tried to make my tea cozy appear scruffy by sewing a few ends of yarn to the sides of the holes.

Fair isle chart *14 sts x 13 rows*

Work in st st. Each square = 1 st and 1 row. Read RS rows from R to L and WS (purl) rows from L to R.

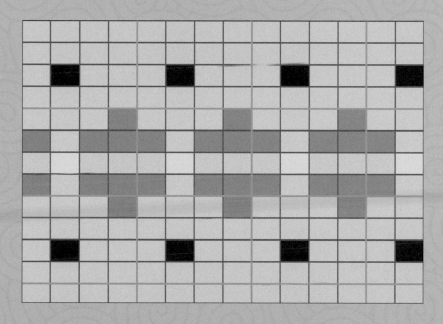

- **A**
- **B**
- **C**
- **D**

A 1950s tea party will come alive with this nostalgic design by Jean Hubbard. Bright, retro colours are a bold and fresh style for your tea table that will not go out of fashion.

Pompom Fancy

Materials

- Stylecraft Special DK (304m/332yd per 100g ball)
- 1 x 100g ball in each of 1205 Apple Mint (A) and 1010 Matador
- NB: Any DK yarn could be substituted
- Pair of 4mm (US6, UK8) knitting needles

Special techniques

- Vertical stripes
- Pompoms – instructions in pattern

Special note

The pleats are formed by each colour being drawn firmly across the back of the colour just used. All strands are carried across on the WS and always carry colours to the end of the rows.

Make 2 pieces

With 4mm needles and A cast on 98 sts and work 7 rows in garter st, ending with RS facing for start of pattern.

Join in B and pattern as follows:

Row 1: K1A, k6B, * k7A, k7B; rep from * to last 7 sts, k6A, k1B.

Row 2: K1B, k6A, * k7B, k7A, rep from * to last 7 sts, k6B, k1A.

These 2 rows form pattern.

Rep rows 1 and 2 until work measures 5½in (14cm) from beg, ending with row 2 and RS facing for next row.

Shape top

Row 1: A k2tog, B k3, k2tog * A k2tog k3 k2tog, B k2tog, k3, k2tog, rep from * to last 7 sts, A k2tog k3, B k2tog (70 sts).

Row 2: B k1, A k4, *B k5, A k5, rep from * to last 5 sts, B k4, A k1.

Row 3: A k2tog, B k1 k2tog *A k2tog k1 k2tog, B k2tog k1 k2tog, rep from * to last 5 sts, A k2tog k1, B k2tog (42 sts).

Row 4: B k1, A k2 *B k3, A k3, rep from * to last 3 sts, B k2, A k1.

Row 5: A k2tog, B k1, *A k2tog k1, B k2tog k1, rep. from * to last 3 sts, A k2tog, B k1 (28 sts).

Row 6: B k1, A k1, *B k2, A k2; rep. from * to last 2 sts, B k1, A k1.

Row 7: (A k2tog) twice, *B k2tog, A k2tog; rep from * to last 4 sts (B k2tog) twice (14 sts).

Break off yarn and thread through rem 14 sts, draw up tightly and fasten off securely.

Making up

Do not press. Join the side seams leaving openings for the handle and spout of the teapot.

Pompoms

Make one red and one green:

Cut 2 circles of stiff card 3½in (9cm) in diameter, then cut out a small circle – about 1–1½in (2–3cm) in the centre. Wind long lengths of wool around the card until the centre hole is almost full. Starting at the top of the circle cut the wool all the way round the circle so that when cut the pompom is held by the centre hole. Do not remove the card at this point. Take a length of the same coloured wool and tie it round the middle of the pompom and secure it very tightly with a knot (leave enough length to use for attaching to the tea cozy). Carefully remove the card. Take the pompom in your hands and gently roll it to create a ball. Attach both the pompoms to the top of the tea cozy.

This tea cozy by Gina Woodward uses fresh spring colours to show an intricate scene of a badger deep in the bluebell wood and a fox among the foxgloves all garlanded by primroses.

Springwatch

Materials

- Jaeger Baby Merino DK (120m/130yd per 50g ball)
- 1 x 50g ball in each of Pale Green (A) and Primrose (B)
- Jaeger Matchmaker DK (120m/130yd per 50g ball)
- 1 x 50g ball in each of Bluebell (C) and Winter White (D)
- Small amounts of same yarn in Black (E), Grey (F), Dark Green (G), Mid Green (H) and Mustard (J).
- Debbie Bliss Alpaca Silk DK (approx 65m/71yd per 50g ball)
- 1 x 50g ball in Russet (K)
- Small bits of 4 ply yarn in 3 hues of pink for the foxgloves
- Jaeger Siena 4 ply cotton – for lining (140m/153yds per 50g ball) 1 x 50g ball
- A pair of 2.75mm (US2, UK12) double-pointed needles.
- A pair each of 3.75mm (US5, UK9) (plus 1 spare) and 2.75mm (US2, UK12) needles.

Tension

22 sts and 30 rows to 4 in (10cm) square using 3.75mm needles.

Special abbreviations

KT = knot: using C, cast on 2 sts, cast off 2 sts, all into same st. Also used for badger's eyes in D, and fox's eyes in J.

Special techniques used

- Intarsia – see page 149
- Fair isle – see page 149

Before commencing

Wind off separate balls of yarn as follows:
3 each in D and E
2 each in C and A

Method

Using 3.75mm needles cast on 56 sts in A. Work in k1, p1 rib for 3 rows.

Next row (WS): Knit.

Begin with a knit row, work 2 rows st st. Now work rows 1–8 inclusive of chart A, using Fair isle method and rep the 8 sts 7 times along row, to form primrose border.

Now work 24 rows of chart B, using intarsia method for fox, A for either side of fox, and approx 30in (76cm) lengths of H for foxglove stems.

At end of 24 rows, leave sts on spare needle, breaking off yarn.

Work second piece in same way, following chart C for 24 rows, again using intarsia method for badger and separate balls of yarn for bluebells either side.

Next row: Using A (but continuing to work foxglove stems in H knit across all 56 sts, then across 56 sts of first piece.

Next row: Purl across all 112 sts.

Commence shaping

Row 1: *K5, k2tog, rep from * to end.

Row 2 and foll alt rows: Purl.

Row 3: *K4, k2tog, repeat from * to end. Continue decreasing in this manner to 32 sts, ending with a purl row.

Next row: K1 *yn fwd k2tog, repeat from * to last st, k1.

Next row: Purl.

Now work 7 rows of chart A, commencing with row 2, rep the 8 sts 4 times across the rows.

Next row (WS): Knit.

Beg with knit row, work 8 rows of st st, then cast off.

Foxgloves
Buds

Make 2 or 3 for top of foxglove stems. Using size 2.75m needles and pink 4 ply, cast on 2 sts.

Row1: Knit, inc in both sts.

Rows 2 & 4: Purl.

Row 3: Knit, inc in first and last st.

Row 5: K2tog 3 times.

Row 6: P3tog.

Cut off yarn leaving enough to sew up side seam and attach to cozy, threading yarn through rem st to fasten it off.

Gloves

Make 4, 5 or even 6 in appropriate pink 4 ply yarn.

Using 2.75mm needles, cast on 12 sts.

Row 1: P1, slip next 2 sts p-wise, p9.

Row 2: Sl 1 p-wise, k2, sl 1 p-wise, turn.

Row 3: P4, turn.

Row 4: Sl 1 p-wise, k3, sl 1 p-wise, turn.

Row 5: P5, turn.

Row 6: K12.

Row 7: P1, sl 1 p-wise, turn.

Row 8: K2, turn.

Row 9: P2, sl p-wise, turn.

Row 10: K3 turn.

Row 11: P12.

Row 12: K2tog, k to last 2 sts, k2tog.

Row 13: Purl.

Rep last 2 rows until 4 sts rem, ending with a purl row. Then, k2tog twice, sl first st over 2nd and fasten off. Again, leave adequate yarn to sew up seam and attach to cozy.

Lining – make 2 pieces

Using 3.75mm needles and 4 ply Siena, cast on 49 sts. Work in st st for 32 rows.

Shape top

Work as for top of cozy, until 21 sts. Cast off. Sew to inside of cozy, placing knit side of lining to inside of cozy.

Making up

Press cozy lightly under damp cloth. Sew on foxglove flowers and buds, keeping seam to back of work. Sew in all ends. Turn 3 rows of rib at base of cozy over to form hem, and catch down. Rep at top of cozy, with 8 rows st st.

Attach lining, then sew up side seams, leaving gap for handle and spout.

Cord

Using A and 2.75mm double-pointed needles, cast on 2 sts.

Next row (RS): K2 – both sts, now on RH needle *slip both sts to opposite end of needle and transfer this needle to LH, without turning work and taking yarn tightly across back of work, knit same 2 sts again – both sts now on RH needle again. Rep from * until cord measures approx 21in (54cm), k2tog and fasten off. Thread through eyelet holes, to meet in centre of badger.

Bluebell tassels – make 2

Using C and 3.75mm needles, cast on 16 sts.

Row 1: Knit.

Rows 2, 4, 6 & 8 : Purl.

Row 3: K1 *yf, k2tog, rep from * to last st, k1.

Row 5: Knit.

Row 7: Make picot hem by knitting each st along row tog with its corresponding st on cast on edge.

Row 9: K2tog 8 times.

Row 10: P2tog 4 times.

Cut off yarn, leaving enough to sew up side of bell and threading yarn through rem 4 sts, drawing up tightly. Thread a bell onto end of cord, and knot end of cord to secure in place.

Chart A *56 sts x 24 rows*

Work in st st. Each square = I st and I row. Read RS rows from R to L and WS (purl) rows from L to R.

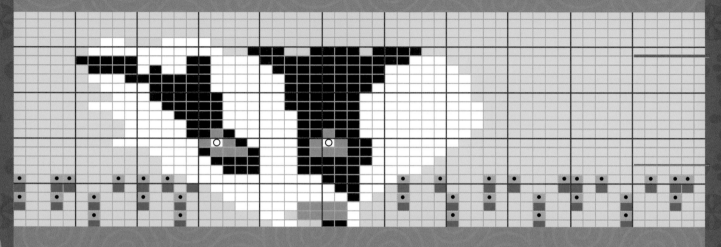

	A		D
	C	⊙	Knot in D
●	Purl in C		E
	Knot in C		F

———— Rejoin pale green at row 19 and gradually fade out all bluebells

———— After row 6, work background in C, knitting placing knots at random

Chart B *56 sts x 24 rows*

Work in st st. Each square = 1 st and 1 row. Read RS rows from R to L and WS (purl) rows from L to R.

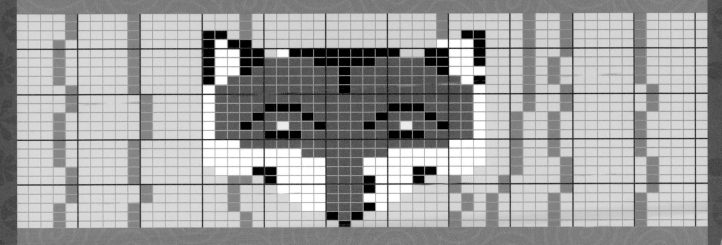

	A
	D
	E

	Knot in J
	K
	H *Use strands of approx 76 cm (30in) for full length stems*

Chart C *8 sts x 8 rows*

Work in st st. Each square = 1 st and 1 row. Read RS rows from R to L and WS (purl) rows from L to R.

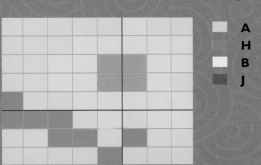

	A
	H
	B
	J

This design by Maud Tabron is a celebration of everything fuzzy, woolly and snuggly. It could be knitted in any colour scheme, but looks great here in the delicate beige and mauve combination.

Woolly Mammoth

Materials

- Sirdar's Curly Wurly (50m/55yd per 50g ball)
- 2 × 50g balls in 068 (Brown) (A)
- Hayfield's Baroque
- 1 × 100g ball in Mauvy Pink (B)
  Note: a spikey fashion yarn can be used for A and a chunky chenille for B
- A pair of 6.5mm (US10.5, UK3) needles

Tension

11.5 sts and 17 rows to 4in (10cm) square on 6.5mm needles.

Linings – make 2

Using 6.5 mm needles and B, cast on 31 sts. Work in st st for 16 rows.

Shaping Rows

Row 1: K1, *k2tog, k8; rep from * to end (28 sts).
Rows 2–4: St st.
Row 5: K1, *k2tog, k7; rep from * to end (25 sts).
Row 6–8: St st.
Row 9: K1, *k2tog, k6; rep from * to end (22 sts).
Rows 10 & 12: Purl.
Row 11: K1, *k2tog, k5; rep from * to end (19 sts).
Row 13: K1, *k2tog, k4; rep from * to end (16 sts).
Rows 14–16: St st.
Row 17: K1, *k2tog, k3; rep from * to end (13 sts).
Row 18: Purl.
Row 19: K1,*k2tog, k2 rep from * to end (10 sts).
Row 20: *P1, p2tog; rep from * to last st, p1 (7 sts).
Row 21: K1, k2tog 3 times (4 sts).

Tip

The contrasting lining looks great here and could be varied with many different colourways. Why not try swapping a knitted lining for a fabric one?

Row 22: P1, (purl into the front and back of the next st) twice, p1 (6 sts).
Row 23: Knit into the front and back of every stitch (12 sts).
Row 24: Purl.
Cast off.

Fronts – make 2

Using 6.5 mm needles and A, cast on 31 sts. Work the 2 fronts following the same pattern as for the linings but using reversed st st instead of st st. (Purl the odd rows, and knit the even rows.)

Making up

Sew each front to a lining with the right sides facing outwards. Then sew the 2 pieces together at the top and bottom of the sides, leaving holes for the spout and the handle.

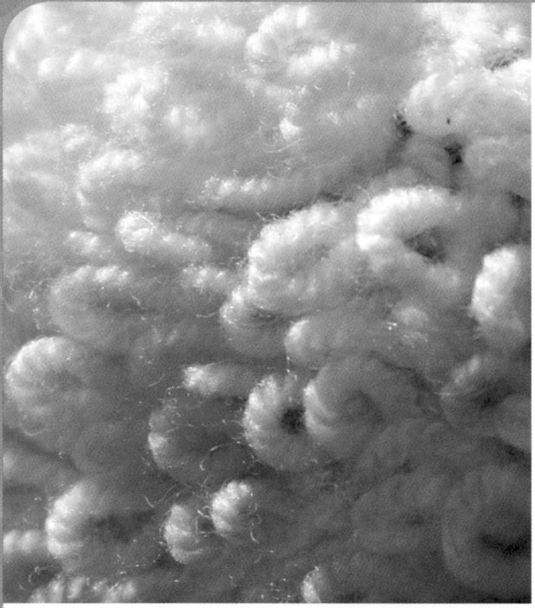

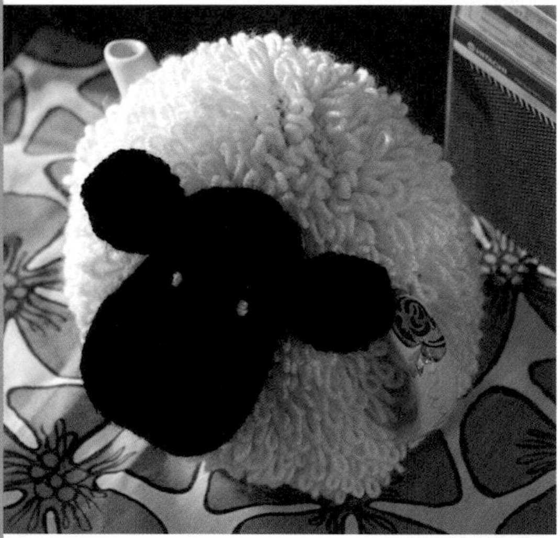

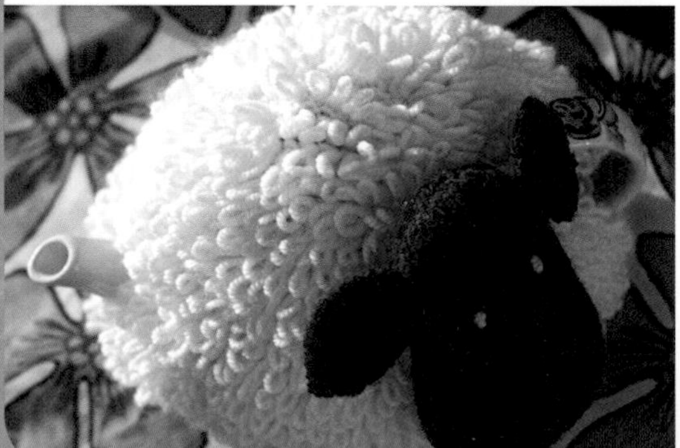

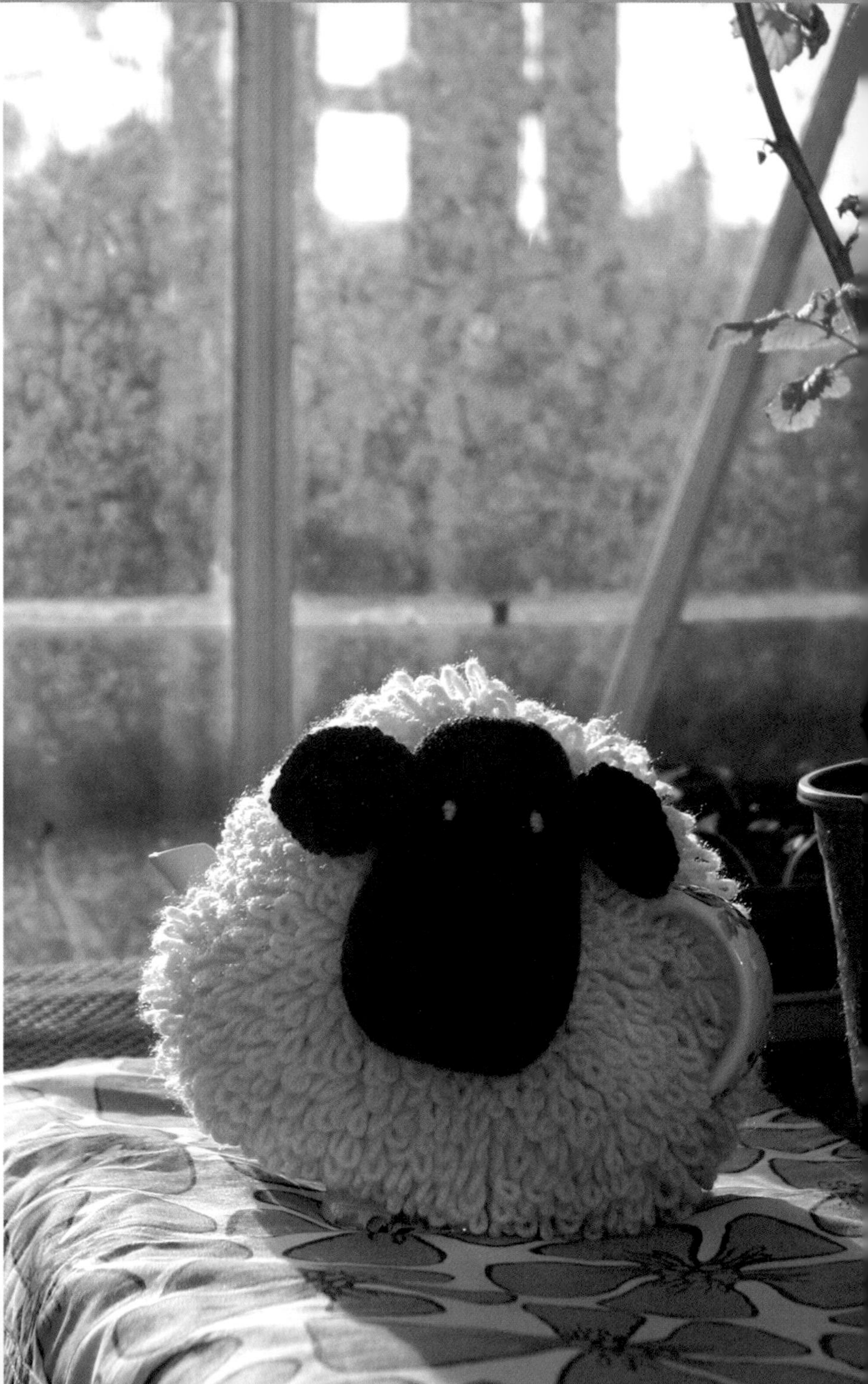

This comical character by Caroline Lowbridge is perfect for warming the pot. The lovely loopy stitch is so effective and really makes a snuggly cozy.

Sheepish Look

Materials

- King Cole Fashion Aran (200m/218yd per 100g ball)
- 2 x 100g balls in 46 Natural (A)
- 1 x 100g ball in 48 Black (B)
- A pair of 4mm (US6, UK8) needles

Special techniques

- Loop stitch – see page 146
- Single rib – see page 145

Body – make 2

With A cast on 44 sts and work 5 rows in single (k1, p1) rib.

Row 6: Knit.

Row 7: K1, *ML, rep from * to last st, k1.

Rows 8 to 29: Rep rows 6 and 7, 11 times, forming loop pattern.

Row 30: K2tog, *k1, rep from * to last st, k2tog (42 sts).

Row 31 and all foll odd rows: As row 7.

Row 32: K2tog, *k1, rep from * to last st, k2tog (40 sts).

Row 34: K2tog, *k1, rep from * to last st, k2tog (38 sts).

Row 36: K2tog. *k1, rep from * to last st, k2tog (36 sts).

Row 38: K2tog, k9 k2tog, k10 k2tog, k9 k2tog (32 sts).

Row 40: K2tog, k8 k2tog, k8 k2tog, k8 k2tog (28 sts).

Row 42: K2tog, k6 k2tog, k8 k2tog, k6 k2tog (24 sts).

Row 44: K2tog, k5 k2tog, k6 k2tog, k5 k2tog (20 sts).

Row 46: K2tog, k4 k2tog, k4 k2tog, k4 k2tog (16 sts).

Row 48: * K2tog, rep from * to end (8 sts).
Cast off.

Head – make 2

With B cast on 6 sts.

Row 1: Inc 1 st into each st across the row (12 sts).

Row 2 and foll even rows: Purl.

Row 3: Inc 1 st into each st across the row (24 sts).

Row 5: K1, m1 k to last st, m1, k1 (26 sts).

Rows 7, 9, 11 & 13: Knit.

Row 15: K1, k2tog, knit to last 3 sts, k2tog, k1 (24 sts).

Row 17: Knit.

Row 19: K1 k2tog, knit to last 3 sts, k2tog, k1 (22 sts).

Row 21: Knit.

Row 23: K1, k2tog, knit to last 3 sts, k2tog, k1 (20 sts).

Row 25: Knit.

Row 27: K1, k2tog, knit to last 3 sts, k2tog, k1 (18 sts).

Rows 29, 31 & 33: Knit.

Row 35: K1, k2tog, knit to last 3 sts, k2tog, k1 (16 sts).

Row 37: K1, k2tog, knit to last 3 sts, k2tog, k1 (14 sts).

Row 39: K1, k2tog, knit to last 3 sts, k2tog, k1 (12 sts).

Row 40: P1, p2tog, p to last 3 sts, p2tog, p1 (10 sts).
Cast off.

Ears – make 2

With B cast on 4 sts.

Row 1 and all foll odd rows: Knit.

Row 2: Inc 1, knit to last st, inc 1, (6 sts).

Row 4: Inc 1, knit to last st, inc 1, (8 sts).

Row 6: Inc 1, knit to last st, inc 1, (10 sts).

Row 8: K4, inc 1, inc 1, k4 (12 sts).

Row 10: K5, inc 1, inc 1, k5 (14 sts).

Row 12: K5, k2tog, k2tog, k5 (12 sts).

Row 14: K4, k2tog, k2tog, k4 (10 sts).

Row 16: K2tog, k6, k2tog (8 sts).

Row 18: K2tog, k4, k2tog (6 sts).

Row 20: K2tog, k2, k2tog (4 sts).
Cast off.

Making up

With loop sides out, put front and back body pieces around chosen teapot and mark openings for spout and handle with safety pins. Join seams, apart from these openings. Sew bound off edges of the ears onto one of the head pieces. Now sew the front and back head pieces together, so the ear join is concealed in the seam. Leave small opening to stuff with washable toy stuffing, or old scraps of fabric or yarn. Sew opening together. With A yarn, sew eyes onto sheep using satin stitch. Stitch length of yarn through back of head, leaving two long ends. Stitch these ends onto the sheep body to fix in place.

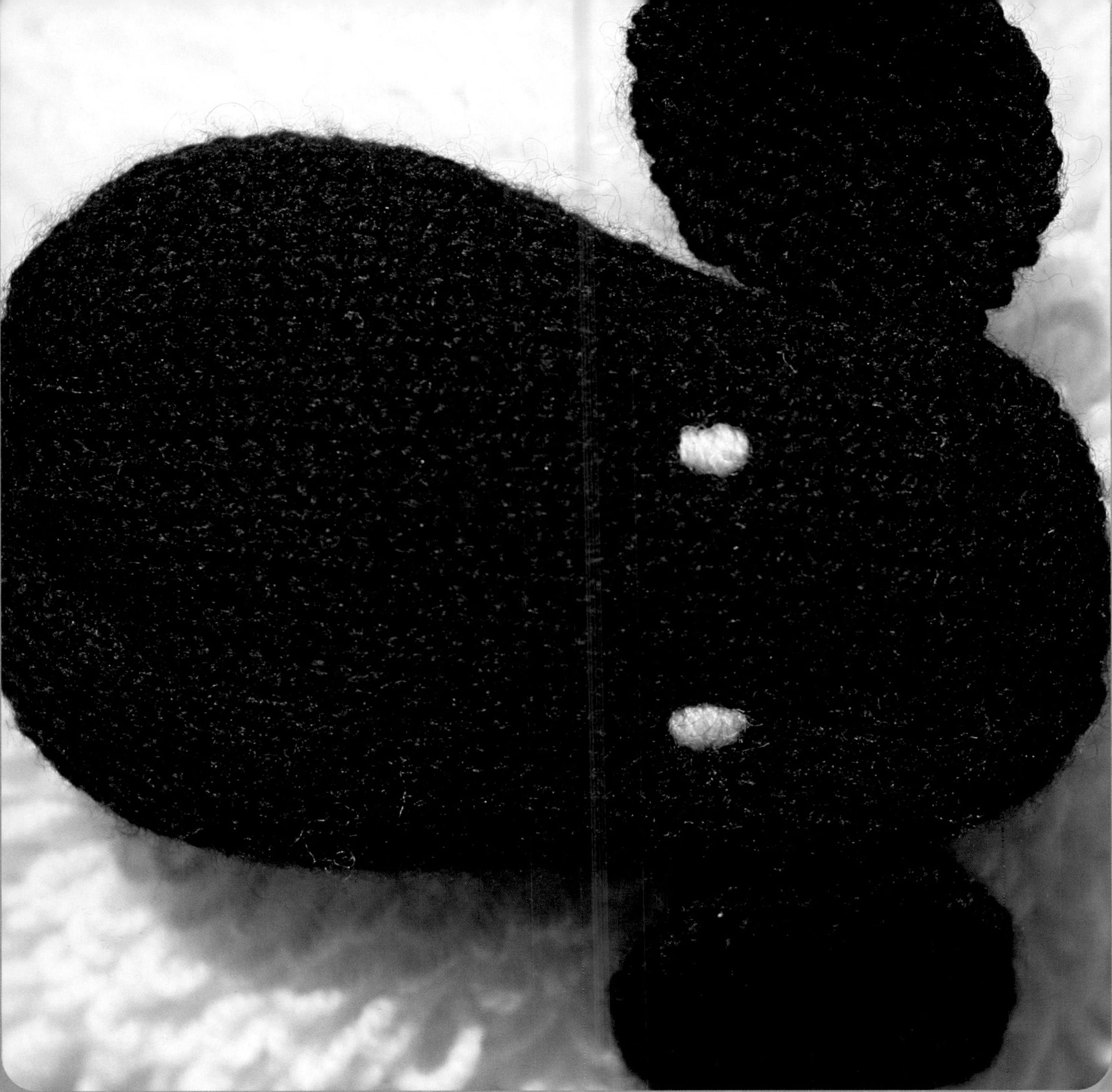

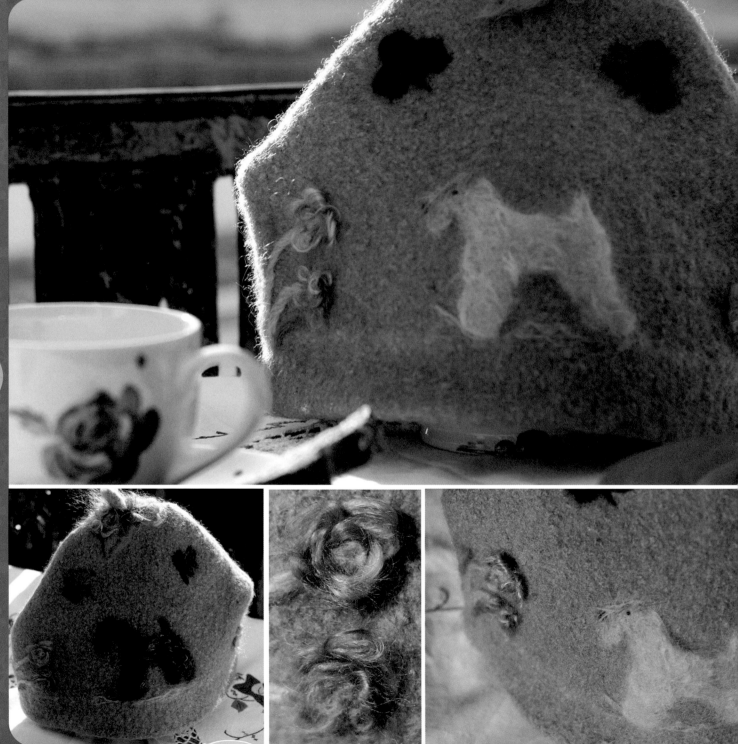

This felted cozy by Tammie Pearce uses soft colours that really evoke a sense of warmth and homeliness. Use your imagination and decorate with your own personal touch.

Country Kitchen

Materials

- Crystal Palace Yarns Iceland (99m/109yd per 100g ball)
- 2 x 100g balls 7063 Dutch Blue
- Oddment of 5329 Celadon (optional)
- 2 x 10mm (US15, UK000) circular needle, 16in (41cm) long
- 5mm (USH, UK6) crochet hook, tapestry needle, felting needles (36 and 40 gauge)
- Felting sponge or block
- Straight pins (for securing pattern to work area)
- Silhouettes of a dog breed, centre cut out to produce a stencil

- Fibre, bits of yarn or wool from many sources, some dyed for felting the decorations on cozy after knitting and machine or hand felting the cozy.
- Two small button eyes appropriate size for the dog breed you have chosen, or other figures

Special techniques

- Chain stitch – see page 150
- Felting – instructions in pattern
- Needle felting – instructions in pattern

Cozy

When felted, the cozy will be approx 10in (25cm) high and 13in (33cm) wide Using one of the circular needles, cast on 92 sts, placing a marker on the needle after the 46th st and at beg of the row. Be careful not to twist sts, knit every row. At 3in (7.5cm) a contrasting row can be added. When the knitting is 11in (28cm) long from beg, start dec as follows: Before and after the 2 st markers k2 tog on every other row until the overall length from beg is 18in (46cm). There will be 34 sts left on the needles, 17 stitches between the markers. Turn inside out and place 17 sts on another circular needle. Use 3-needle cast off and cast off all stitches to form the top of the cozy. If you would like the cozy to be larger cast on more stitches and work more rows.

Loop

Using crochet hook, make 16 chain. Attach securely to middle of the top of the cosy and weave in the end around the loop three times to make the loop thicker and the base a bigger attachment. Weave in all loose ends before felting.

Felting

Use very hot water and put cozy in a fastened pillowcase to protect the washing machine. Place small amount ($\frac{1}{2}$ tspn) of liquid soap or detergent on the pillowcase and place in the washing machine on high agitation. Check the progress of the felting process every 5–10 minutes and continue to agitate until the piece has felted to your liking. Hand felting can also be done but may require more patience.

Rinse with cool water when felting is complete to remove the rest of the soap. Roll the finished felted cosy in towels to remove most of the moisture and then lay out to dry. Shaping should be done at this point. If your teapot has decorative sides or is particularly round, the felt will stretch at this point and can be shaped to fit your particular teapot.

Needle felting

Once dry, take a silhouette of the dog breed you prefer and cut out the centre of the silhouette carefully. This will leave the white portion of the paper as a stencil. Put the stencil portion on the felt fabric with the fibre or wool under the paper. Secure the paper with straight pins to the felting surface or felting block.

Do not worry that the fibre or wool extends beyond the stencil edges.

To needle felt to the fabric, hold a felting needle straight up and down. Poke the needle through the yarn and fabric, working along its length until the yarn is firmly felted to the underlying fabric.

Begin by needle felting the edges of the dog first and then work in slowly to attach the fibre to the felt. Carefully lift up small sections of stencil and fold the excess fibre or wool into the centre of the pattern, felting as you go around the outside edge. Add fibre anywhere it seems necessary or to obtain the look you would like.

Add any flowers or other felted decorations freehand as you like with coloured or natural fibre or wool. Sew on button eyes and the tea cozy is complete.

Dog template - *actual size*

This reversible tea cozy by Frankie Brown has its own knitted-in mat. A choice of spots or stripes makes a versatile accessory – button it on and it is transformed into designer wear for the modern teapot.

Spots and Stripes

Materials
- Rowan Cotton Glacé (15m/124yd per 50g ball)
- 2 × 50g balls in Navy 746 (A)
- 1 × 50g ball in each of Blue 810 (B), Gold 802 (C) and Red 741 (D)
- A pair of 3.25mm (US3, UK10) needles
- 2 × circular 3.25mm (US3, UK10) needles
- 4 × ½in (15mm) buttons

Tension
11.5 sts and 18 rows to 4in (10cm) square on fronts using 7.5 mm needles.

Special techniques
Fair isle – see page 149
Single rib – see page 145

The tea cozy is knitted in one long strip then folded and knitted up into the finished shape on circular needles. This means that there is very little sewing up.

Stripes

With A cast on 34 sts.
Work in st st, changing colour every 2 rows and foll the colour sequence A, B, C, D. Carry yarns loosely up the side. Work 34 rows in this stripe pattern, thus ending with 2 rows in A.

Base

The base is worked in A throughout.
Row 1: Sl1 k-wise *k1, yb sl1 p-wise, rep from * to last st, k1.
Row 2: Sl1 p-wise, purl to end.
Work this 2 row pattern until 38 rows have been worked in total. Now work another 32 rows in the stripe pattern as before, following the colour sequence D, C, B, A.
K2 rows in A. *(This will mark the top of the finished cozy.)*

Spots

Work 2 rows st st in A followed by 2 rows garter st.

Spot pattern 1

Row 1: B k1 *sl2 p-wise, k4, rep. from * to last 3 sts, sl2 p-wise, k1.
Row 2: P1, *sl2 p-wise, p4, rep from * to last 3 sts, sl2 p-wise, p1.
Rep. these 2 rows twice more then work 2 rows garter st in A.

Spot pattern 2

Row 1: C k4, *sl2 p-wise, K4, rep. from * to end.
Row 2: P4, *sl2 p-wise, p4, rep. from * to end.
Rep these 2 rows twice more then work 2 rows g-st in A.
Work these two spot patterns twice more using the colour sequence D, B, C, D. Use separate strands for each colour pattern.
Finish spot panel with 2 rows st st in A.

Base

Work base in the same way as before. 2 rows garter stitch in A.
Now work 6 spot patterns as before, following the colour sequence D, C, B, D, C, B.
2 rows st st in A.
Cast off and weave in ends.

Handle ribbing

With RS facing and a circular needle, pick up and knit 108 sts down one long side, picking up 20 sts for each pattern panel and 14 sts for each base.
Fold the long strip in half, positioning half the picked-up sts at each end of the circular needle.
Holding the two ends of the circular needle together in one hand and a straight 3.25mm needle in the other, work 54 sts in single (k1, p1) rib. You will be working the sts on the circular needles together as you go in a technique similar to that used in a three-needle cast off.
Now work back and forth in k1,p1 rib in the normal way, dec 2 sts in the middle of first and every alternate row by working the centre 4 sts as ssk and k2tog until 42 sts rem.
Cast off in rib.

Spout ribbing

Work as for handle ribbing, but don't cast off.

Button band

Work 6 rows in single (k1,p1) rib on first 10 sts. Cast off these 10 sts in rib.

Buttonhole band

Rejoin yarn to rem 32 sts and cast off 22 sts.

Rib to end, work one more row in k1, p1 rib on these 10 sts.

Next row: Rib 5 sts, cast off 2 sts, rib to end.

Next row: Rib 3 sts, cast on 2 sts, rib to end.

Work 2 more rows in rib and then cast off in rib.

There will be one short seam remaining to sew together. Using A, oversew this together now.

Top ribbing

Using a circular needle and beginning with the button flap, pick up and knit 80 sts round top, picking up 10 sts for the button and buttonhole bands, 24 sts for each pattern repeat and 6 sts for each section of handle rib. This will join the tea cozy above the handle while keeping the spout side open.

Work 2 rows k1,p1 rib.

Next row: Rib 3, cast off 2 sts, rib to end.

Next row: Rib 75 sts, cast on 2 sts, rib to end.

Work 5 more rows in rib.

Cast off in rib and weave in ends.

Sew on 4 buttons back to back on both sides of the button band.

This cozy by Pam Soanes was inspired by Swaledale sheep, the fleece of which were traditionally used in carpet making. The looped pile and matching lining provide excellent insulation.

Loopy Lamb

Materials

- British Breeds Jacob Aran
- 3 x 100g balls in Cream (A)
- 1 x 100g in Grey (B)
- 1 pair 4.5mm (US7, UK7) needles
- Black tapestry wool to embroider the eyes and nose
- A small quantity of washable stuffing or wadding for the nose
- A stitch holder, a safety pin large enough to hold 7 sts and a blunt-ended needle for sewing up

Tension

- 18 sts and 24 rows to 4in (10cm) square in st st.
- 15 sts and 26 rows to 4in (10cm) square in loop stitch.

Special techniques

Loop stitch – see page 146

Back head

Using 4.5mm needles and A, cast on
42 sts.

Row 1: Purl

Row 2: (K1, loop 1) to end, K1.

Rep last 2 rows 14 more times, marking
either end of row 9 to assist with sewing
up (30 rows).

Row 31: Marking either end of this row
with contrasting yarn, (p1, p2tog) 5 times,
p12, (p2tog, p1) to end (32sts).

*Row 32 and every alt row: As row 2.

Row 33: (P6, p2tog) to end (28sts).

Row 35: (P5, p2tog) to end (24sts).

Row 37: (P4, p2tog) to end (20sts).

Row 39: (P3, p2tog) to end (16sts).

Row 41: (P2, p2tog) to end (12sts).

Row 42: This will be decreasing and
casting off at the same time. P2tog twice.
Pass first loop over second, (p2tog, pass
prev st over) to end*.

Front head

As for back until 3 loop rows have been
knitted.

Row 7: P5, knit twice into next st (for
selvedge). Put these 7 sts on to a safety
pin. (They will later be used to knit the
RH side of the face.) Cast off 30 sts p-
wise (should leave 1 st on RH needle
and 5 sts on LH needle. Purl twice into
next st, purl to end (7sts on needle).

Row 8: K1, loop 5 sts, k1.

Row 9: Purl.

Row 10: As Row 8

Rows 11-22: As rows 9 and 10
(6 times).

Row 23: Inc 1 st, purl to end of row.

Row 24: K1, loop 6, k1.

Row 25: Cast on 2 sts, purl to end
of row.

Row 26: K1, loop 8, k1.

Row 27: As row 25.

Row 28: K1, loop 10, k1.

Row 29: Cast on 4 sts, purl to end
of row.

Row 30: K1, loop 14, k1.

Put these 16 sts on to a stitch holder.
Replace the 7 sts held on a safety pin on
to the needle such that you can
commence work with RS facing. Rejoin
yarn and knit the LH side of face to
match, rows 8–30, reversing the shapings
such that the inc are at the end rather
than the beginning of the row.

Row 31: P1, p2tog to end, cast on 10 sts
and then cont across the 16 sts for the
RH side, left on a stitch holder, (p1,
p2tog) to last st, p1. You should now have
32 sts on the needle. And the 2 sides of
the face should be joined.

Rows 32–43: As given for back.

Face

Using B and 4.5mm needles, cast on
36 sts. (NB: This does not correspond
to the number of sts left in the front
head because of the difference in tension
between st st and loop stitch.)

Rows 1–15: Starting with a knit row,
work 15 rows in st st.

Row 16: K2tog, k to last 2 sts, k2tog,
marking the 18th stitch with contrasting
yarn to guide the positioning of the nose.

Rows 17–22: Continue in st st, casting
off 2 sts at beg of next 2 rows, 4sts at
beg of next 2 rows, and then 5 sts at beg
of foll 2 rows (12 sts).

Row 23: Cast off p-wise.

Nose

With A and 4.5mm needles, cast on 32
sts.

Rows 1–6: Starting with a knit row, work
in st st.

Row 7: K2tog to end (16sts).

Row 8: Purl

Rows 9–12: Rep rows 7 and 8 twice
more (4sts).

Leaving a long enough tail to sew on the
nose, cut the yarn and pull through the
remaining 4 sts to secure.

Eyes – 2 pieces

These are worked from the top down.
With Aran and 4.5mm needles cast on
5 sts.

Row 1: Working in st st, start with a
purl row.

Row 2: Inc 1 st at both ends.

Row 3: Purl.

Row 4: With RS (k side) of work facing,
inc 1 st at beg of row.

Rows 5–6: Cont to inc 1 st at same side

of work as in row 4 (10sts on needle).

Row 7: Dec 1 st at beg of row, purl.

Row 8: Knit, dec 1 st at end of row.

Row 9: Purl, dec 1 st at both ends.

Row 10: Knit to last 2 sts, k2tog.

Cast off p-wise, marking the last st with contrasting yarn. This indicates the bottom outside corner of the eye where it will be sewn to the face edge.

Make another eye, reversing the shaping.

Ears – 4 pieces

With B and 4.5mm needles, cast on 6 sts.

Starting with a knit row, k2 rows in st st.

Row 3: Inc 1 st at each end, knit.

Row 4: Purl.

Rep the last 2 rows twice more.

Rows 9–11: Cont straight in st st on 12 sts.

Rows 12–16: Cont in st st, dec 1 st at each end of every row.

Row 17: K2tog and pass yarn through rem loop to secure.

Make 3 more the same.

Lining – 2 pieces

Using A and 4.5mm needles, cast on 50 sts (more than for the outside because of the difference in the tension).

Rows 1–4: K1, p1 rib.

Rows 5–28: In st st, starting with a knit row.

Row 29: (K1, k2tog) 6 times k12, (k2tog, k1) 6 times, (38 sts).

Row 30 and each foll alt row: Purl.

Row 31: (K7, k2tog) 4 times, (34 sts).

Row 33: (K6, k2tog) 4 times (30 sts).

Row 35: K2tog, k3, k2tog, (k5, k2tog) twice, k4, k3tog (24 sts).

Row 37: K4, k2tog, (k3, k2tog) twice, k4, k2tog (18 sts).

Row 39: K3, k2tog, (k2, k2tog) twice, k3, k2tog.

Row 41: Dec and cast off simultaneously: K2tog, k2tog, pass first loop over second, **k2tog, pass previous loop over. Rep from ** to end.

Making up

Block out and very lightly steam all the stocking stitch pieces to facilitate sewing up. Fit the face into the front head and pin to hold in place. Sew together, fitting it close to the 'roots' of the loops. The best finish is achieved by sewing with the right side facing you.

Join the two straight edges of the nose. Line up the point on the outer, curved edge immediately opposite the seam you have just made with the marker on the face. That seam should then be at the bottom centre edge of the face.

Pin the outer edge to the face in an approximate circle, so that the nose takes a cone shape, and sew to the face leaving sufficient room to insert stuffing. Stuff firmly and sew up the gap.

With the cast-off edge of the eyes at the top, position the eyes at the outer corners of the face and sew on. Using tapestry yarn double, embroider the eyes and nose as shown using a simple straight stitch. Make up the ears by seaming the outer edges, but leaving the bottoms open. Put aside.

Using the markers of contrasting yarn as a guide, sew up the two looped outer sides of the cozy leaving an opening between the markers for the handle and spout. Sew the two sides of the lining together in the same way. Take a thread through the top centre of the lining and through the top centre of the outer cozy. The inside of the lining should show the knit side. Pull through to help position the lining and secure. Sew the lining to the outer cozy at the bottom edges and at the spout and handle gaps.

Next fix the ears. Tuck the bottom ⅜in (1cm) of each ear into itself to make a firm base. Fold each ear along its length and catch in this position with a stitch at the base. Position the ears on the seam of the outer cozy and secure.

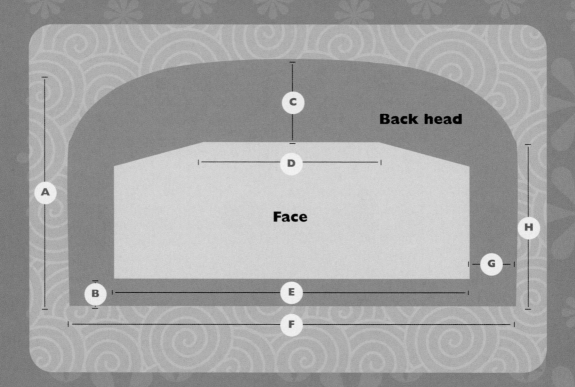

Back head

Face

A	6½in (16.5cm)	E	8in (20cm)
B	1in (2.5cm)	F	11in (28cm)
C	2in (5cm)	G	1½in (4cm)
D	2½in (6cm)	H	4½in (11cm)

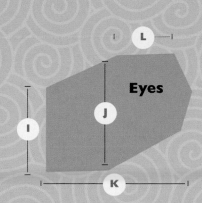

Eyes

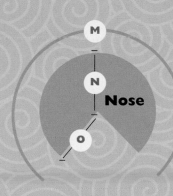

Nose

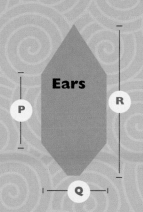

Ears

Eyes

- **I** 1¼in (3cm)
- **J** 1½in (4cm)
- **K** 2in (5cm)
- **L** ¾in (2cm)

Nose

- **M** 9½in (24cm)
- **N** 2in (5cm)
- **O** 1½in (4cm)

Ears

- **P** 1in (2.5cm)
- **Q** 2¼in (6cm)
- **R** 3in (8cm)

This show-stopping tea cozy was designed by Maud Tabron – inspired by her tea-loving and ballroom-dancing grandmother who taught her to knit. A glittering addition to any tea table.

Glitter Ball

Materials
- James C Brett's Chunky Marble (220m/240yd per 100g ball)
- 1 x 100g ball in MT3 Turquoise Mix (A)
- James C Brett's Aran Denim
- 1 x 100g ball in Turquoise Green (B)
- A pair of 6.5mm (US10.5, UK3) needles
- You will also need beads or buttons for decoration
  (You could use beads from old necklaces that can be bought cheaply in charity shops.)

Special techniques
Double rib – see page 145

Linings – make 2

Using 6.5 mm needles and 3 strands of B held together, cast on 31 sts.
Work in st st for 12 rows.

Shaping rows

Row 1: K1, *k2tog, k8, rep from * to end (28 sts).
Rows 2–4: St st.
Row 5: K1, *k2tog, k7, rep from * to end (25 sts).
Rows 6–8: St st.
Row 9: K1, *k2tog, k6, rep from * to end (22 sts).
Row 10: Purl.
Row 11: K1, *k2tog, k5, rep from * to end (19 sts).
Row 12: Purl.
Row 13: K1, *k2tog, k4, rep from * to end (16 sts).
Rows 14–16: St st.

Row 17: K1, *k2tog, k3, rep from * to end (13 sts).
Row 18: Purl.
Row 19: K1, *k2tog, k2, rep from * to end (10 sts).
Row 20: *P1, p2tog; rep from * to last st, p1 (7 sts).
Row 21: K1 (k2tog) 3 times (4 sts).
Row 22: P1, work into the front and back of the next 2 sts, p1 (6 sts).
Row 23: Knit into the front and back of every st (12 sts).
Row 24: Purl.
Cast off.

Fronts – make 2

Using 6.5 mm needles, 2 strands of A and 1 strand of B, cast on 38 sts. Work in double rib (k2, p2 etc) for 12 rows.

Shaping rows

Row 1: *K2, p2tog, k2, p2, rep from * to last 6 sts, k2, p2tog, k2 (33 sts).
Row 2: *P2, k1, p2, k2, rep from * to last 5 sts, p2, k1, p2.
Row 3: *K2, p1, k2, p2, rep from * to last 5 sts, k2, p1, k2.
Row 4: *P2, k1, p2, k2, rep from * to last 5 sts, p2, k1, p2.
Row 5: *K2, p1, k2, p2tog; rep from * to last 5 sts, k2, p1, k2 (29 sts).
Row 6: *P1, k1, rep from * to last 2 sts, p2.
Row 7: *K2, p1, rep from * to last 2 sts, k2.
Row 8: *P1, k1, rep from * to last 2 sts, p2.
Row 9: *K2tog, p1, rep from * to last 2 sts, k2tog, (19 sts).
Row 10: *P1, k1, rep from * to last st, p1.
Row 11: *K1, p1, rep from * to last st, k1.

Row 12: *P1, k1, rep from * to last st, p1.
Row 13: *K1, p1, rep from * to last st, k1.
Row 14: *P1, k1, rep from * to last st, p1.
Row 15: *K1, p1, rep from * to last st, k1.
Row 16: *P1, k1, rep from * to last st, p1.
Row 17: *K1, p1, rep from * to last st, k1.
Row 18: *P1, k1, rep from * to last st, p1.
Row 19: *K2tog, rep from * to last st, k1 (10 sts).
Row 20: *P1, p2tog, rep from * to last st, p1 (7 sts).
Row 21: K1 (k2tog) 3 times (4 sts).
Row 22: P1, work into the front and back of the next 2 sts, p1 (6 sts).
Row 23: Knit into the front and back of every stitch (12 sts).
Row 24: Purl.
Cast off.

Making up

Sew beads down the furrows made by the rib. Then sew each front to a lining with the right sides facing outwards. Sew the 2 pieces together at the top and the bottom of the sides, leaving holes for the spout and the handle.

Vibrant green makes an attractive meadow backdrop for the peacefully grazing cow and sheep decorations on this design by Hazel Wagstaff. The basic shape could be used to inspire many other variations.

Green Goddess

Materials

- Rowan Rowanspun DK (200m/218yd per 50g ball)
- 1 x 50g ball in each of 747 Green (A) and 738 Grey (B)
- A pair of 5.5mm (US9, UK5) needles
- Small flower beads
- A selection of animal buttons

Tension

18 sts and 32 rows to 4in (10cm) square over garter st using yarn double.

Size

Instructions given for regular and large tea pots with variation for a taller pot.
The larger size is given in brackets.
Regular size – holds 1.5 pints – approx 5in (12cm) tall.
Large size – holds 2.5 pints – approx 6in (15cm) tall.

Note

Yarn is used double throughout.

Main body – make 2

Meadow Frill

Using A and 5.5mm needles cast on 141[157] sts.

Row 1: K1, *k2, lift first of these 2 over 2nd, rep from * to end.

Row 2: Purl.

Row 3: As row 1.

Change to B for dry stone wall.

Row 4: Purl.

With RS facing, work 6[10] rows reverse st st beg purl row.

Variation: For a taller tea pot an extra even number of rows may be added here.

With RS facing, rejoin A and proceed in g-st for remainder of hill and knit 28 rows.

Commence decrease:

Large size only: *K8, k2tog rep from * to end. Knit 1 row.

Both sizes: *K7, k2tog rep from * to end (32 sts).

Next and every foll alt row: Knit.

Next row: *K6, k2tog rep from * to end.

Next row: *K5, k2tog rep from * to end.

Next row: *K4, k2tog rep from * to end.

Next row: *K3, k2tog rep from * to end.

Next row: *K2, k2tog rep from* to end.

Next row: *K1, k2tog rep from* to end.

Next row: K2 tog across the row (4 sts).

Draw yarn through and fasten off.

Making up

Place both pieces with RS together. Sew up green frill for meadow and grey stone wall sections on both sides. Leave side of green hill open until beginning of decrease. Continue sewing up from this point to the top of the hill on both sides. Turn to right side. Alternatively – pin both pieces together. Place over teapot. Mark openings for handle and spout. Sew up accordingly. Attach flower beads and animal buttons as required.

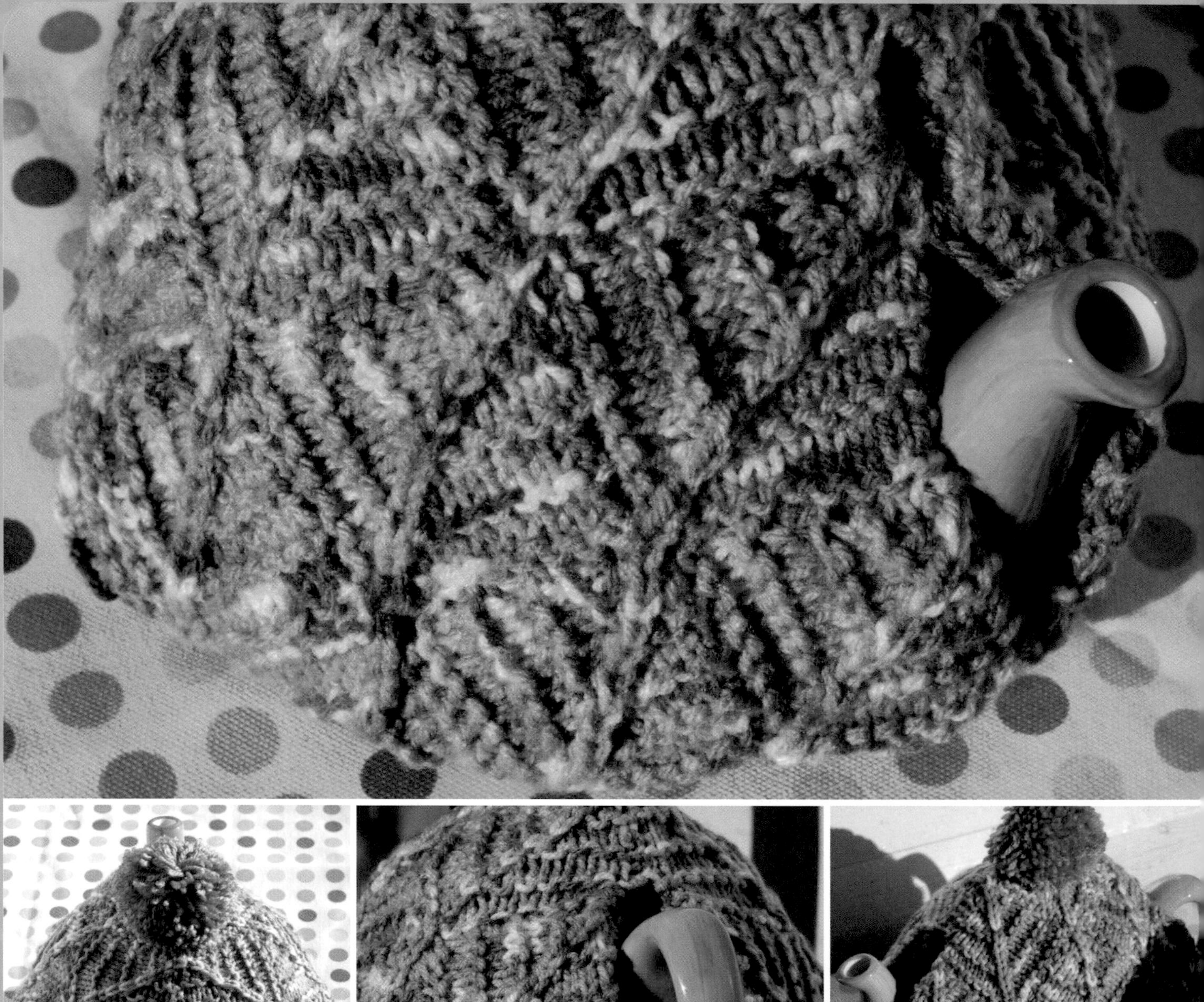

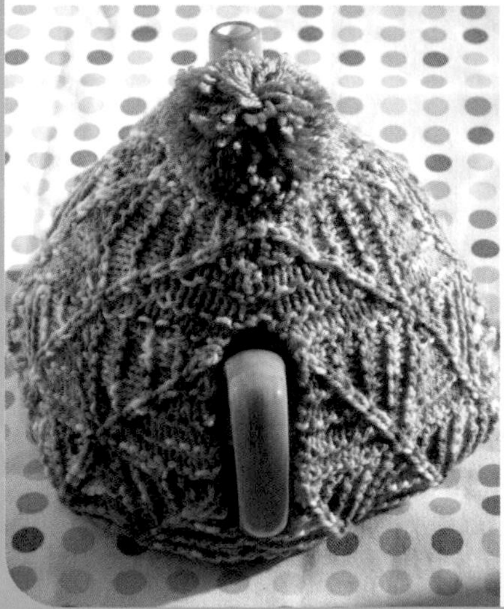

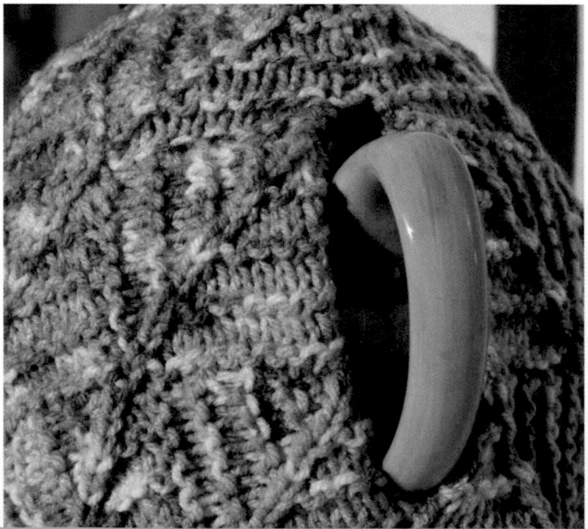

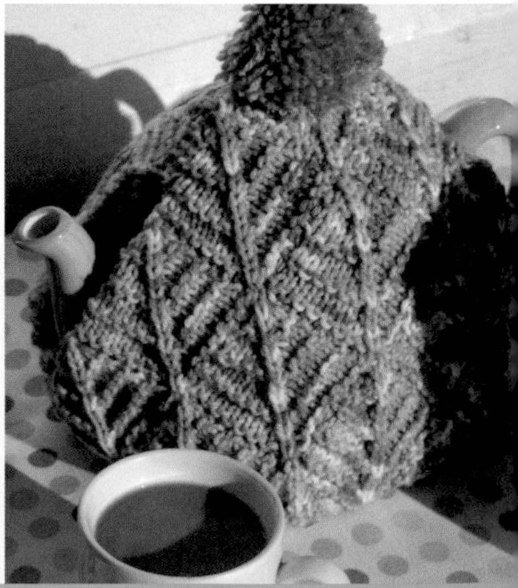

This design by Maud Tabron is a modern twist on a traditional tea cozy. It uses the modular knitting technique which is particularly good when working with space-dyed yarn.

Tea Squares

Materials

- Sirdar Bonus Flash DK (280m/306yd per 100g ball)
- 1 x 100g ball in each of 907, Blue and White Mix (A) and 969 Blue (B).
- A pair each of 4mm (US6, UK8) and 6.5mm (US10.5, UK3) needles.

Special techniques

- Mitred squares – instructions in pattern
- Pompoms – see page 60

Linings – make 2

Using 6.5mm needles and 3 strands of B held together, cast on 31 sts quite loosely. Work in st st for 12 rows.

Shaping Rows

Row 1: K1, *k2tog, k8; rep from * to end (28 sts).
Rows 2–4: St st.
Row 5: K1, *k2tog, k7; rep from * to end (25 sts).
Rows 6–8: St st.
Row 9: K1, *k2tog, k6; rep from * to end (22 sts).
Row 10: Purl.
Row 11: K1, *k2tog, k5; rep from * to end (19 sts).
Row 12: Purl.
Row 13: K1, *k2tog, k4; rep from * to end (16 sts).
Rows 14–16: St st.
Row 17: K1, *k2tog, k3; rep from * to end (13 sts).
Row 18: Purl.
Row 19: K1, *k2tog, k2; rep from * to end (10 sts).
Row 20: *P1, p2tog; rep from * to last st, p1 (7 sts).
Cast off.

Fronts – make 2

Using 4mm needles and A, work the squares and triangles indicated on the diagram using the mitred square modular technique.

Basic square
Square 1

Row 1: Using 4mm needles and yarn A cast on 19 sts.
Row 2: (WS) K9, p1, k9.
Row 3: K8, slip 2 sts tog, k1, pass slipped sts over tog, (from now on shown as S2kp2) k8 (17 sts).
Row 4: Purl.
Row 5: K7, S2kp2, k7 (15 sts).
Row 6: K7, p1, k7.
Row 7: K6, S2kp2, k6 (13 sts).
Row 8: Purl.
Row 9: K5, S2kp2, k5 (11 sts).
Row 10: K5, p1, k5.
Row 11: K4, S2kp2, k4 (9 sts).
Row 12: Purl.
Row 13: K3, S2kp2, k3 (7 sts).
Row 14: K3, p1, k3.
Row 15: K2, S2kp2, k2 (5 sts).
Row 16: K2, p1, k2.
Row 17: K1, S2kp2, k1 (3 sts).
Row 18: P3tog.
Fasten off or leave stitch on the needle to use as the first st of the next square.

Square 2

Using 4mm needles and A pick up and k9 sts from the L side of square 1, and then cast on 10 sts (19 sts). Work as for square 1, starting with row 2.

Square 3

As square 1.

Square 4

Using 4mm needles and A pick up and k9 sts from the L side of square 3, cast on 1 st, and then pick up and k9 sts from the R edge of square 1 (19 sts). Work as for square 1, starting with row 2.

Square 5

Using 4mm needles and A pick up and k9 sts from the L side of square 4, pick up and k1 st from the top of the centre ridge of square 1, and then pick up and k9 sts from the R edge of square 2 (19 sts). Work as for square 1, starting with row 2.

Square 6

As square 1.

Square 7

Using 4mm needles and A pick up and k9 sts from the L side of square 6, cast on 1 st, and then pick up and k9 sts from the R edge of square 3 (19 sts). Work as for square 1, starting with row 2.

Square 8

Using 4mm needles and A pick up and k9 sts from the L side of square 7, pick up and k1 st from the top of the centre ridge of square 3, and then pick up and k9 sts from the R edge of square 4 (19 sts). Work as for square 1, starting with row 2.

Square 9

Using 4mm needles and A pick up and k9 sts from the L side of square 8, pick up and k1 st from the top of the centre ridge of square 4, and then pick up and k9 sts from the R edge of square 5 (19 sts). Work as for square 1, starting with row 2.

Square 10

Using 4mm needles and A cast on 10 sts, and pick up and k9 sts R side of square 6 (19 sts). Work as for square 1, starting with row 2

Square 11

Using 4mm needles and A pick up and k9 sts from the L side of square 10, pick up and k1 st from the top of the centre ridge of square 6, and then pick up and k9 sts from the R edge of square 7 (19 sts). Work as for square 1, starting with row 2.

Square 12

Using 4mm needles and A pick up and k9 sts from the L side of square 11, pick up and k1 st from the top of the centre ridge of square 7, and then pick up and k9 sts from the R edge of square 8 (19 sts). Work as for square 1, starting with row 2.

Basic triangle
Triangle 13
Row 1: Pick up 19 sts as for a square (9 + 1 + 9).
Row 2: K9, p1, k9.
Row 3: K2togtbl, k6, S2kp2, k6, k2tog (15 sts).
Row 4: Purl.
Row 5: K2togtbl, k4, S2kp2, k4, k2tog (11 sts).
Row 6: K5, p1, k5.
Row 7: K2togtbl, k2, S2kp2, k2, k2tog (7 sts).
Row 8: P3tog, p1, p3tog (3 sts).

Row 9: S2kp (1 st).
Fasten off.

Triangle 14
As triangle 13, but worked downwards.

Triangle 15
As triangle 13, but worked downwards.

Making up

Sew in any ends. Sew each front to a lining with the right sides facing outwards. Then sew the 2 pieces together at the top and the bottom of the sides, leaving holes for the spout and the handle.

Make a pompom

See page 60 for instructions. Use the end of yarn left over from tying, to secure the pompom to the top of the tea cozy.

Country folk will love this rural scene designed by Claudia Lowe. Rugged stone walls, blue sky and green fields dotted with sheep make a timeless and quintessential country view.

Counting Sheep

Materials

- Jamieson Shetland 2 ply (115m/125yd per 25g)
- Oddments in rust (A), Light Brown (B), Sea Green (C), Dark Blue (D), Off White (E), Pale Yellow (F), Light Blue (G), Pale Grey (H)
- 50g of one colour is needed for the lining
- A length of black yarn is needed for embroidery
- A pair of 4mm (US6, UK8) needles
- Some toy stuffing or a small piece of wadding

Tension

24 sts and 28 rows to 4in (10cm) square over st st using 4mm needles and 2 strands of yarn together.

Special techniques

- Reverse stocking stitch – purl on RS, knit on WS
- Intarsia – see page 149
  NB: *Use two strands of yarn throughout.*

Tea cozy – make 2

With 4mm needles and I strand of A and I of B, cast on 52 sts.

Rows I and 2: Knit.

Row 3: *K4, p4, rep from * to end.

Row 4: *P4, k4, rep from * to end.

Rep rows 3 and 4 once.

Row 7: *P4, k4, rep from * to end.

Row 8: *K4, p4, rep from * to end.

Rep rows 3–8 once more. Then rep rows I and 2. Break off yarns.

With I strand of C and I of D, work from the chart. Using intarsia method, work the sheep in E in rev st st while working the grass in st st. After row 6, break off and use F. When you have completed the chart, break off F. Using 2 strands of C, work 2 rows of garter st (every row knit).

Work 2 rows st st using I strand of G and I of E. Then work 4 rows in E and H.

Shape top

Next row: K2tog all along the row.

Next row: Purl.

Rep the last two rows once. Draw the yarn tightly through the remaining sts and fasten off.

Lining – make 2

Using 4mm needles and 2 strands of lining colour, cast on 52 sts.

Work two rows g-st.

Work 44 rows in st st.

Shape top as for cozy.

Making up

Using black yarn, embroider faces and legs on sheep as shown. Stitch together the two pieces of the cozy for 6 rows at the base. Seam the upper parts above the work from the chart. Seam the lining pieces in the same way, leaving 2 gaps. Stitch the lining to the cozy around the two gaps. Put a little toy stuffing or wadding in each side between the lining and the cozy. Stitch around the base, securing the lining to the cozy. Catch the lining and cozy together at the top.

Rose – make 5 petals

Petal: Using 4mm needles and 2 strands of E, cast on 2 sts.

Next row: Knit, inc in each st (4 sts).

St st 3 rows, inc I st at each end of every row.

Next row: KI, * k2tog, yo, rep from * to last st, kI.

Next row: Purl.

Next row: K3tog, 3 times, kI.

Break off yarn and pull thread through sts and fasten off.

Stitch sides of petals together. Sew ends of petals to top of cosy over the gap at the top.

Counting Sheep Chart *18 sts x 52 rows*

Work in st st. Each square = 1 st and 1 row. Read RS rows from R to L and WS (purl) rows from L to R.

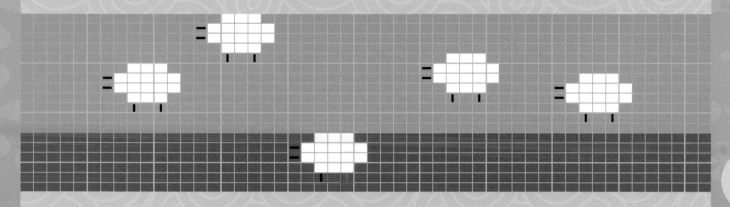

	St st with C and D		Reverse st st with C and E
	St st with D and F	**I**	Embroidery with black

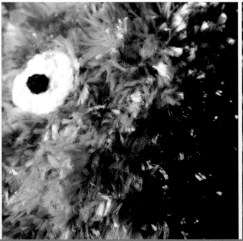

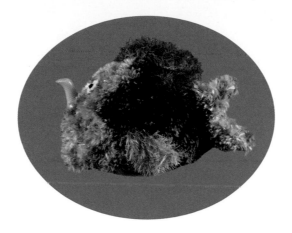

This funky fish cozy by Joyce Meader uses furry yarn to create
a fluffy texture and bright colours to ensure that this design
is bursting with cheeky character.

Funky Fish

Materials

- Fun fur look yarn (approx DK)
- 2 x 50g balls in each of Pink (A), Blue (B)
- 1 x 50g ball in Pink Blend (C)
- Smooth DK
- Oddments in White (D) and Black (E)
- A pair of 4mm (US6, UK8) needles
- 3mm (USD, UK11) Crochet hook

Special techniques

- Intarsia – see page 149
- Double crochet – see page 150

Main body – make 2

With 4mm needles cast on 36 sts in A, 24 sts in B (60 sts total).

Work in intarsia technique as chart, remembering to weave in yarn when changing colours to prevent gaps.

Dec for top:

Next row: *K2tog, k3 rep from * to end.

Next row: Work 1 row.

Next row: *K2tog, k2 rep from * to end.

Next row: Work 1 row.

Next row: *K2tog, k1 rep from * to end.

Next row: Work 1 row.

Next row: *K2tog rep from * to end.

Next row: Work 1 row.

Cast off.

Small fin – make 2

Using C, cast on 12 sts and work 1 row.

Next row: K2tog, work to last st, inc 1.

Next row: Inc 1 st, k9 sts, k2tog.

Work these 2 rows 5 times (10 rows).

Cast off and leave length of yarn to attach fin to main body.

Large fin – make 1

Using C, cast on 20 sts and work 1 row.

Next row: K2tog, work to last st, inc 1.

Next row: Inc 1 st, work 17 sts, k2tog.

Work these 2 rows 5 times (10 rows).

Work 1 row.

Next row: k2tog, work to last st., inc 1.

Next row: Inc 1 st, work 17 sts, k2tog.

Work these 2 rows 5 times (10 rows).

Work 1 row then cast off.

Fold over and sew together open short ends. Leave long edge open to attach to top of main body closing the opening.

Tail – make 2

Using A cast on 20 sts and work 4 rows in garter st.

Next row: K9 k3tog, knit to end.

Working on first 9 sts:

Next and every foll alt row: Knit.

Next row: K7 k2tog.

Next row: K6 k2tog.

Next row: K5 k2tog.

Next row: K4 k2tog.

Next row: K3 k2tog.

Next row: K2 k2tog (3 sts).

Next row: K3tog.

Re-join yarn at centre and complete the other side with first dec row on first row: K2tog k7.

Next row: Knit 1 row etc.

Eyes – make 2

Using 3mm crochet hook work a white circle in dc until 1in (2.5cm) across. Work a large French knot in black in centre of eye. You can make the eye from white felt and embroider a black centre.

Making up

Sew up main body leaving holes for the handle and spout. Attach eyes and fins. Make sure that the pattern is symmetrical on both sides to look like a fish.

Funky Fish Chart *60 sts x 36 rows*

Work in st st. Each square = 1 st and 1 row. Read RS rows from R to L and WS (purl) rows from L to R.

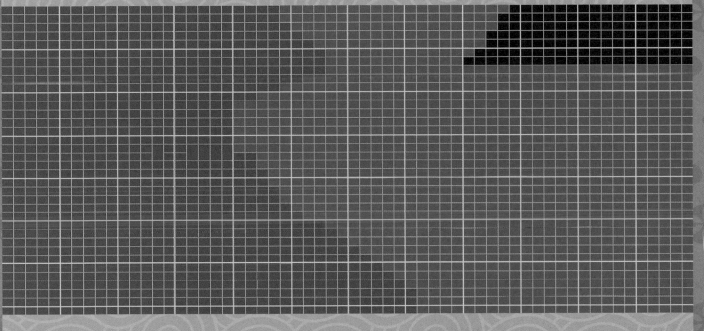

 A
B
C

Wrap up your tea pot in this cozy cardigan by Sara Thornett.
These chunky, hearty cables will make sure your tea stays
piping hot so everyone can enjoy a second cup.

Warm Hug

Materials

- Rowan Yorkshire Tweed Chunky
  (100m/109yd per 100g ball)
- 2 × 100g per ball, shade 551
- A pair of 7mm (US10.5, UK2) needles
- Cable needle
- 4 × 7mm (US10.5, UK2) double-pointed needles
- 5 × ½in (12mm) brown, woven leather buttons

Special techniques

- Cables – see page 146
- Single rib – see page 145

Cabled body – make 2

Work 2 alike from bodies chart using 7mm needles and cable needle.

Handle sleeve

Using 7mm needles cast on 39 sts and starting with a p st, work 3 rows single (p1, k1) rib.

Commence broken rib patt thus:

Row 1: Knit.

Row 2: K1, *p1, k1, rep from * to end. These 2 rows form patt and should be rep 8 times in all.

Next row: Knit and cast off.

Spout sleeve

Using 7mm needles cast on 15 sts and starting with a p st, work 3 rows single (p1, k1) rib.

Commence broken rib as given for handle sleeve and rep the 2 rows throughout at the same time after first knit row, inc 1 st at each edge, work 2 rows. Keeping broken rib patt correct throughout, dec 1 st at beg of every row until 2 sts rem. K2tog and fasten off.

Circular base

Using 7mm double-pointed needles cast on 6 sts. Split sts between 3 needles, use 4th needle to knit first round (6 sts).

Round 2: M1 into every st, 12 sts.

Next and foll 8 alt rounds: Knit

Round 4: *M1, k1, rep from * to finish (18 sts).

Round 6: *M1 K2, rep from * to finish (24 sts).

Round 8: *M1 K3, rep from * to finish (30 sts).

Round 10: *M1 K4, rep from * to finish (36 sts).

Round 12: *M1 K5, rep from * to finish (42 sts).

Round 14: *M1 K6, rep from * to finish (48 sts).

Round 16: *M1 K7, rep from * to finish (54 sts).

Round 18: *M1 K8, rep from * to finish (60 sts).

Round 20: Loosely cast off all 60 sts.

Making up

Once all pieces are completed sew together using blunt needle and tweed yarn, attaching circular base last. When linking this to 'bodies', allow for overlap at meeting points also care and judgement need to be used to ensure the longer length of the 'bodies' base fits to half of the circular base circumference. Sew on buttons. No buttonholes are needed as buttons can be pushed through the cable knit itself. Extra room in the handle 'sleeve' allows for the hand to hold the teapot handle when pouring the tea.

Cabled Bodies *51 sts x 41 rows*

Work in st st. Each square = 1 st and 1 row.

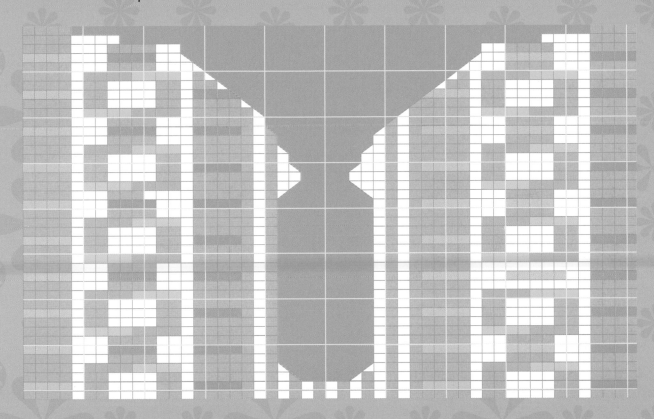

	Knit on RS, purl on WS	**Cable A** Sl 2 st to cn, hold cn forward, k2, k 2 from cn.
	Purl on RS, knit on WS	
	Cable A	**Cable B** Sl 2 st to cn, hold cn back k2, k2 from cn.
	Cable B	
	Cable C	**Cable C** Sl 2 st to cn, hold cn forward, p2, k2 from cn.
	Cable D	
	Decrease stitch	**Cable D** Sl 2 st to cn, hold cn back, k2, p2 st from cn.

Keep your cuppa steaming with this tea cozy by Debbie Gore knitted in hot pinks and purples. With the natural warmth of merino wool — this design has a feeling of richness and indulgence.

Colourful Cables

Materials
- Louisa Harding Kashmir Aran (91m/99yd per 50g ball)
- 2 × 50g balls in 10 (A)
- Debbie Bliss Merino Chunky (65m/71yd per 50g ball)
- 2 × 50g balls in colour 14072 (B)
- Debbie Bliss Merino Aran (90m/100yd per 50g ball)
- 1 × 50g ball in each of 325001 (C), 325606 (D) and 325702 (E)
- One pair each of 3.25mm (US3, UK10), 4mm (US6, UK8), 5mm (US8, UK6) needles
- Cable needle

Tension
18 sts and 25 rows to 4in (10cm) square measured using 5mm needles and st st.

Special abbreviations
(CB) = slip next 3 sts on to a cable needle and leave at the back, knit the next 3 sts, then knit the 3 off the cable needle. Follow cols as in pattern.

Special techniques
- Cables — see page 146
- Intarsia — see page 149

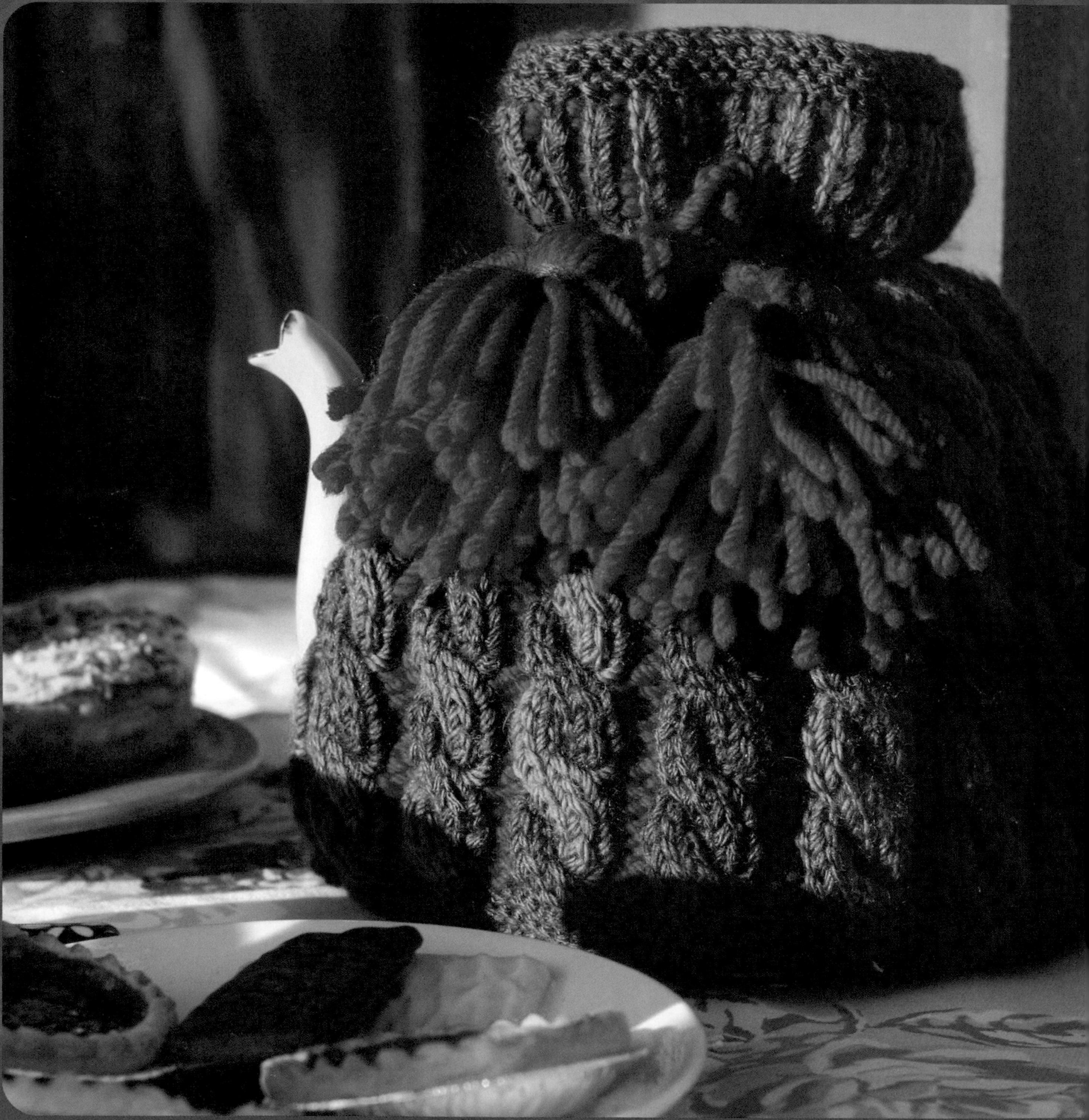

Special note

This pattern may look complicated but is easy to do if you make sure that each stitch is knitted the same colour as previously, even when twisted with the cable. That is the colours swap sides after each cable twist. Use the intarsia method of knitting with small balls or long lengths of wool for each section.

Outer cozy – make 2

Using 3.25mm needles and A, cast on 66 sts and knit 4 rows.

Break off A, change to 4mm needles and using the intarsia method of knitting, join in the colours as shown on the cable chart. Work from colour and cable chart repeating the 12 rows twice more. Then repeat cable row 3.

Next row: (Dec row) Change to A and 3.25mm needles and *p2tog along the row (33sts).

Next row: Knit.

Next row: Purl.

Eyelet row: K2 * yo, k2tog, k2, rep from * to last 3 sts, yo, k2tog, k1.

Starting with a purl row, work 3 rows st st.

Break off A and join in colours as striped rib chart, knitting all sts on first row.

Next row: Knit all the B sts and purl the rest to form a single rib.

Rib the next 6 rows in cols as set.

Change to A and knit 4 rows.

Cast off.

Lining– make 2

Using A and 4mm needles cast on 45sts and knit 4 rows.

Change to 5mm needles and st st. Shape the sides by dec at each end of 7th and every foll 6th row to 33 sts.

Cont in st st until length matches the front to the dec row.

Change to 3.25mm needles and work 2 rows st st.

Eyelet row: K2 * yo, k2tog, k2, rep from * to last 3 sts, yo, k2tog, K1.

Starting with a purl row, work 3 rows st st.

Change to 4mm needles.

Joining in short length of B, knit as follows: 2A, * 1B, (leave yarn at front) 3A, rep to last 2 sts 2A.

1st row: Keeping cols as set, p2A, * put RH needle, k-wise through next st, cross A over B, k st with B, p3A, rep to last 2 sts, p2A.

2nd row: K2A, * put RH needle through next st p-wise, cross A over B, p st using B, K3A, rep to last 2 sts, k2A.

Rep these 2 rows twice more and first once.

Knit 4 rows garter st in A.

Making up

Press cable sections over a towel. Press lining sections. Join side seams of the outside cover, leaving room for the spout and handle. Join side seams of the lining in the same way. Slip stitch the lining inside the cover. Make a cord or crochet chain approx 18in (46cm) long. Thread through eyelet holes. Make and attach tassels to either end and tie in a bow.

Striped Rib Chart *33 sts x 7 rows*

Read RS rows from R to L and WS rows from L to R.

Work in st st. Each square = 1 st and 1 row.

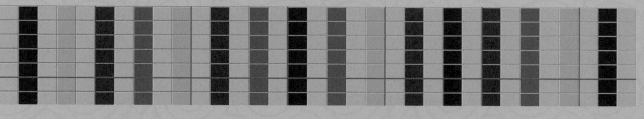

A
B
C
D
E

Cable Pattern Chart *12-row repeat*

Read RS rows from R to L and WS rows from L to R.
Work in st st. Each square = 1 st and 1 row.

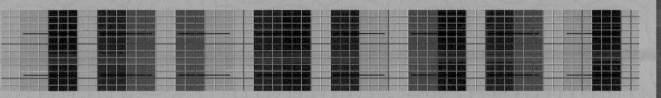

A
C ⎤
D ⎥ Knit on RS (odd rows)
E ⎦ Purl on WS (even rows)

B Purl on RS and knit on WS

Cable positions (CB)
Slip next 3 sts onto cable needle and leave at back
Knit next 3 sts, then knit the 3 off the cable needle

Colourful Cables

This is the dog enthusiast's ideal tea cozy. Based on her Airedale Terrier, this design by Helen Edgar is a fun way to include your beloved dog in the ritual of tea-making.

Tea for Two

Materials

- DK yarn of your choice (approx 175m/191yd per 50g ball)
- 200g green (A), 50g Black (B), 100g Tan (C)
- Pair of 4mm (US6, UK8) needles
- Toy safety eye with washer
- Wadding
- Material (of your choice) to line the inside of the cozy
- Very small amount of stuffing for nose

Front

Using A, cast on 84 sts and knit 2 rows.
Beginning with a knit row, work 2 rows
st st.

Begin following chart from 5th row, thus:

Row 5: K4 (A), k33 (B), k17 (C), k30 (A).

Row 6: P30 (A), p17 (C), p33(B), p4 (A).

Keep foll the chart thus, until row 59 has
been worked.

Keeping chart correct, dec as follows:

Row 60: Dec 1 st at end of row.

Row 61: Dec 1 st at beg of row.

Row 62: Dec 1st at end of row.

Rows 63–77: Dec 1 st at each end of
row.

Rows 79–81: Keep dec 1 st at each end
of rows, but work these rows in g-st.

Cast off rem 43 sts.

Back

Knit a matching piece, but using only (A).

Ear – make 1

Worked in st st throughout. Using (C),
cast on 3 sts and knit 1 row. (This is
bottom point of ear.)

P1 row, inc 1 st at each end.

Carry on in st st, shaping as follows:

Row 3: Inc 1 st at beg of next row.

Row 4: Inc 1 st at end of next row.

Row 5: Inc 1 st at each end of next row.

Row 6: Inc 1 st at beg and 2 sts at end
of next row.

Rows 7, 9, 11, 19: Purl 1 row
(no shaping).

Row 8: Inc 2 sts at beg and 1 st at end
of next row.

Row 10: Inc 1 st at beg of next row.

Row 12: Inc 1 st at each end of next
row.

Row 13, 15, 17: Inc 1 st at end of row.

Rows 14, 16, 18: Knit 1 row (no
shaping).

Row 20: Inc 1 st at beg and dec 1 st at
end of next row.

Rows 21–24: Work straight.

Row 25: Dec 1 st at beg of row.

Work 2 rows straight.

Cast off rem 19 sts.

Sew to face on cozy as indicated in the
photographs, with bottom point of ear
sloping slightly towards the nose.

Eye

A toy safety eye has been used in the
photographic example, but one could be
embroidered with black wool if desired.

Mouth

A mouth can be embroidered in black
wool, if desired.

Nose – make 1

Worked in garter st throughout. With
(B), cast on 5 sts.

Knit 1 row straight.

Shape as follows:

Inc 1 st at each end of following 4 rows.

Work 6 rows straight.

Dec 1 st at each end of next 4 rows.

Cast off rem 5 sts.

Sew a gathering stitch around edge of
nose. Draw in loosely, stuff lightly, draw in
tighter and sew to face, as marked in
photograph.

Making up

Cut lining material to the required size
for each half of the cozy. Do the same
for the wadding. With the wadding in
place, between the lining material and
the knitted piece, sew lining to inside
of each half of cozy. With right sides
(knit) facing each other, sew the tea
cozy together along the side and top
edges, then turn the right way out.

If desired, take a number of strands of
green and black wool (or a contrast of
your choice) and make a cord or plait
with them, ensuring it is long enough
to go along the top and sides (ie. the
outline) of the cozy. When it is complete,
knot each end tightly (so it won't come
undone) and back stitch to the cozy.

Tea for Two Chart *85 sts x 81 rows*

Each square = 1st and 1 row

Read RS rows from R to L and WS rows from L to R.

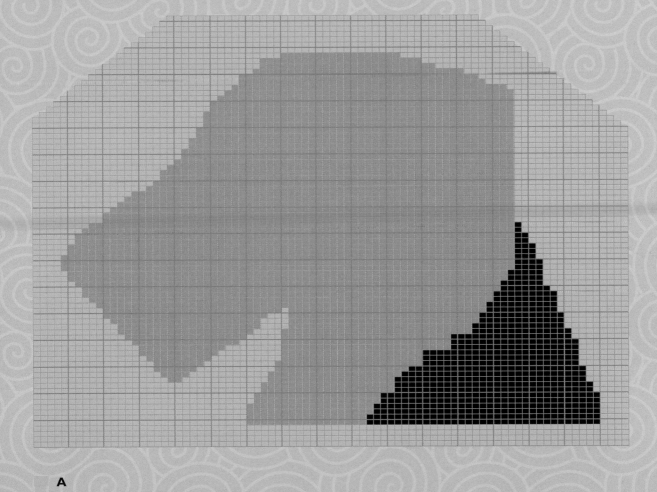

A
B
C

Create an attractive flower arrangement for the tea table with Maud Tabron's pretty design. Use any colour roses you like to suit your own colour scheme.

Tea Rose

Materials

- Sirdar Country Style DK (318m/348yds per 100g ball)
- 1 x 100g ball in SH538 Green (A) (3 strands used)
- James C Brett's Marble (or any Tweed DK yarn)
- 1 x 100g ball (2 strands used) in MT6 Green Multi (B) and oddment for roses (C)
- Richard Poppleton's Sierra (or any lopi chunky yarn)
- 1 x 50g ball in Grey
- Sirdar Snuggly Snowflake DK (any DK yarn with fleecy texture) (170m/186yds per 50g ball)
- 1 x 50g ball in White

- Wendy Corinne (or any brushed DK yarn)
- 1 x 50g ball in White
- A pair each of 4mm (US6, UK8), 6.5mm (US10.5, UK3) and 7.5mm (US11, UK1) knitting needles

Tension

11 sts and 18 rows measure 4in (10cm) square on 7.5 mm needles.

Linings – make 2

Using 6.5mm needles and B (1 strand of grey chunky and 1 strand of tweed double knitting held together), cast on 31 sts. Work in st st for 12 rows.

Shaping rows

Row 1: K1, *k2tog, k8; rep from * to end (28 sts).
Rows 2–4: St st
Row 5: K1, *K2tog, k7; rep from * to end (25 sts).
Rows 6–8: St st.
Row 9: K1, *k2tog, k6; rep from * to end (22 sts).
Row 10: Purl.
Row 11: K1, *k2tog, k5; rep from * to end (19 sts).
Row 12: Purl.
Row 13: K1, *k2tog, k4; rep from * to end (16 sts).
Row 14: Purl
Row 15: K1, *k2tog, k3; rep from * to end (13 sts).
Row 16: Purl.
Row 17: K1, *k2tog, k2; rep from * to end (10 sts).
Row 18: *P1, k2tog; rep from * to last st, p1 (7 sts).
Row 19: K1, k2tog 3 times (4 sts).
Row 20: P1, (purl into the front and back of the next st) twice, p1 (6 sts).
Row 21: Knit into the front and back of every stitch (12 sts).
Row 22: Purl.
Cast off.

Fronts – make 2

Using 7.5mm needles and A (2 strands of green double knitting and one strand of tweed held together), cast on 31 sts. Work the 2 fronts following the same pattern as for the linings.

Making up

Sew each front to a lining with the right sides facing outwards. Then sew the 2 pieces together at the top and the bottom of the sides, leaving holes for the spout and the handle.

Decoration

There are 2 different types of roses.

Rose 1 – make 2

Outer Petals
Using 4 mm needles and brushed DK yarn, cast on 58 sts.
Row 1: Knit.
Row 2: P2, * p2tog, p1; rep from * to last 2 sts, p2 (40 sts).
Row 3: Knit.

Row 4: *P3tog, p1; rep from * to end (21 sts).
Row 5: Knit.
Row 6: *P1, p2tog, p2; rep from * to end (16 sts).
Row 7: Knit.
Row 8: P2tog across the row (8 sts). Thread the yarn through rem sts, tighten up and fasten off.
Inner Petals
Using 4 mm needles and brushed DK, cast on 21 sts.
Row 1: Knit.
Row 2: *P1, p2tog, p2; rep from * to end (16 sts).
Row 3: Knit.
Row 4: P2tog across the row (8 sts). Thread the yarn through rem sts, tighten up and fasten off.
Centre
Using 4 mm needles and brushed DK, cast on 8 sts.
Work in st st for 3 rows.
Next row: P2 tog, p4, p2tog (6 sts). Cast off. Fold round into a cup shape and sew up side seam.

Assemble the rose by joining each piece together. Sew the centre into the inner petals and then onto the outer petals. Sew in any ends, leaving one to sew the rose to the tea cozy.

Rose 2

Using 4 mm needles and fleece DK, cast on 35 sts.

Row 1: Knit.

Row 2: Purl.

Row 3: K1, *k1, m1, k1; rep from * to end (53 sts).

Row 4: Purl.

Row 5: K1, *k2, m1, k1; rep from * to end (71 sts).

Row 6: Purl.

Row 7: K1, *k3, m1, k1; rep from * to end (89 sts).

Row 8: Purl.

Row 9: K1, *k4, m1, k1; rep from * to end, (107 sts).

Cast off.

Wind up the rose into a flower shape and fasten it together. Try to leave an end to sew the rose to the tea cozy.

Leaves – make 6

Using 4 mm needles and green DK, cast on 5 sts.

Row 1: K2, yo, k1, yo, k2 (7 sts).

Row 2: Purl.

Row 3: K3, yo, k1, yo, k3 (9 sts).

Row 4: Purl.

Row 5: K4, yo, k1, yo, k4 (11 sts).

Row 6: Purl.

Row 7: skpo, K7, K2tog (9 sts).

Row 8: Purl.

Row 9: skpo, K5, K2tog (7 sts).

Row 10: Purl.

Row 11: skpo, K3, K2tog (5 sts).

Row 12: Purl.

Row 13: skpo, K1, K2tog (3 sts).

Row 14: Purl.

Row 15: K3tog (1 st).

Fasten off.

Making up

Sew the leaves to the bottom of the roses and then arrange the roses around the top of the tea cozy and sew on. I grouped mine around the spout end.

Idyllic village life is captured perfectly in this design
by Christine Edgar which incorporates crochet details
that really set the scene.

Village Green

Materials

- Jamieson and Smith 2 ply jumper weight Shetland wool (approx 115m/125yd per 25g)
- Oddments in 78 Brown (A) and 202 Cream (B) (for rib and dry-stone wall)
- A mixture of oddments of Rowan yarns, in similar weights to roughly match shades in colour pattern.
- Crochet yarns (all fine cottons) Coats fine cotton: cricket ball 469 bat 625
- Cordonnet Mercer 307 Yorkshire tea-cakes
- Bat handle DMC 320, Pontefract cakes DMC Black, Yorkshire puddings DMC 897
- Rose, any white wool

- Sheep, oddments of black and white wool
  Also it looks good if touches of pinky mauve are added to resemble heather.
- 3.25mm (US3, UK10) circular needle, 16in (40cm) in length.
- A set of 4 × 3.25mm (US3, UK10) double-pointed needles
- 1mm (US10, UK4) and 3mm (USD, UK11) Crochet hook

Special techniques

- Steeks – see pattern notes
- Intarsia – see page 149
- Chain stitch – see page 150
- Double crochet – see page 150

Pattern notes

A steek is a vertical column of stitches – or wrapped loops within the knitting, which will be cut open once the piece of work is knitted. This is a useful technique when working circular knitting and coloured work. Colours can be joined at the steek position simply by knitting the old and the new colours together – the knots will be cut out when the loops are cut through and the ends finished. In this pattern steeks are made by wrapping yarn around the needle then dropping the wraps on the next row – making a series of long loops which are cut through for the handle position and the spout opening.

Pattern

Using 3.25mm needle cast on 100 sts using the thumb method. Using cream and brown, rib k1 brown, p1 cream for 1½in (4cm).

Next row: Inc 22 sts evenly across the row.

Begin steeks.

To make a wound steek, wind wool in use around RH needle several times (I did 7), then carry on knitting as normal. Work the steek at the beginning and do not forget to work it again halfway round. These will later be cut and fastened off. Always drop the wound stitches the next round.

Begin dry-stone wall pattern, remembering to make steeks after 61 sts. Knit 1 row using brown wool.

Row 1: Purl 1 row using brown, inc into first st st then every 4th st until 121 sts.

Row 2: K3 cream wool, slip next st p-wise. Cont halfway, make steek and cont to end. Rep 4 times.

Row 7: Knit using brown wool including all the sts.

Purl 1 row dark.

Then repeat, remembering to start k1 slip 1 dark, k3 light, 1 dark, to bring dark wool in centre of former 3 light sts. Using light and dark wool, k1 dark, k1 light for 1 row then next row k1 light, k1 dark.

Change to straw coloured wool.

Knit 12 rows.

Now begin landscape. *(Remember to lay in wool when changing colours – saves sewing in later. There are a great many ends as yarn will be at wrong end on next round. I cut it off and pulled it free as there would be a terrible tangle otherwise.)*

Round 1: Using light green k11 sts, change to mustard k8, change to dark green k7, change to white k10, change to tweedy green k7, change to mustard k17 *(no need for steek as new colour)*. Using dark green k11, change to mustard k17, change to dark brown k17, then tweedy green k16 sts. Round 1 completed.

The wool is now the wrong end, cut it off and lay in the ends. Cont in patt from chart as set by the first row remembering you will always be reading chart from R to L (RS) and decreasing sts as shown on chart starting on 6th round.

Note: Stop making steeks on 9th round – work will cont all the way around with no 'gaps' from now on. Change to double-pointed needles to cont working in rounds as cozy becomes smaller.

Round 18: Working in cols approx as patt chart, dec sts evenly across the row until 70 sts.

Round 19: Working in cols approx as patt chart, dec sts evenly across the row until 62 sts.

Round 20: Working in cols approx as patt chart, dec sts evenly across the row until 52 sts.

Round 21: Working in cols approx as patt chart, dec sts evenly across the row until 42 sts.

Round 22: Using straw and light green

wool alternately, k3, k2tog across the row.

Round 23: Change to mixed rib alternating cols as set ie. k1, p1, dec evenly across the row until 28 sts.

Rounds 24 & 26: Cont in bi-col rib.

Round 25: Dec 10 sts evenly across the row (18 sts).

Round 26: Rib 1 straw, 1 green.

Round 27: Using straw wool k2tog along the row (9 sts).

Final round: Run threads (2) through all sts.

Crochet items

Yorkshire puddings

Using 1mm hook for all items with the exception of the rose (using size 3mm). Using 1mm hook work 6 ch, join with a sl st to make a ring.

Round 2: 2ch (as first dc), 11 dc into ring.

Round 3: 2ch (as first dc), 1dc in same dc, * 1ch, 2dc in next dc, rep from * ending 1ch, sl st to 2nd of 2ch.

Cont as set by round 3. When it is as big as you think Yorkshire puds should be, make the next round tighter by missing out the ch sts and fasten off.

Pontefract cakes

Using 1mm hook work 5 ch, join with a sl st to make a ring.

Work as for puds. Size is smaller than puds. It is a matter of choice.

Tea cakes

As puds but sewn on in reverse. Brown currants embroidered with brown straight stitches afterwards.

Cricket ball

As teacakes.

Cricket bat

Using 1mm hook and cream work 7 ch, turn.

Round 1: Work 1dc into each ch, 1ch, turn and work back along other side of ch and work 1 dc in bottom of each ch to end, 1ch, sl st to first dc.

Round 2: 1ch (as first dc), 1dc in each dc to end, 3dc in ch sp, 1 dc in each dc from round 1 at other side, ending sl st to first dc.

Round 3: Sl sl over first 2 sts, work as round 2 to last 2 sts.

Handle

Change to green and work 3dc into top edge of bat. Cont to work dc on these sts until required length. Fasten off.

Rose

Make a small inner rose: Using 3mm hook work 9 ch and sl st into a circle. Go around the circle making 1 dc 3 tr 1 dc 5 times. Fasten off. Set aside.

Outer circles:

Round 1: Using 3mm hook and white make 12 ch. Join with a slip st.

Round 2: 1 ch 12 dc into ring, sl st to 1st ch.

Round 3: 1 ch, beg in same st as 1 ch, (1dc 3ch miss 1 st)5 times, sl st to 1st dc.

Round 4: (petals) 1 ch, work 1dc, 3ch, 5tr, 3ch, 1dc, into each ch lp of previous round, sl st to 1st dc.

Round 5: 1 ch, (1 dc between dc, 5ch, behind petals of previous round) sl st to 1st dc.

Round 6: (petals) 1 ch, (1dc, 3ch, 5tr, 3ch, 1dc) into each ch lp of previous round sl st to 1st dc.

Fasten off.

Embroider or sew a small motif to the centre if desired.

Finishing touches

Work sheep using white French knots with straight black sts for legs and a black knot for nose.

Village Green Chart *121 sts x 21 rows*

Work in st st. Each square = 1 st and 1 row. Read RS rows from R to L and WS (purl) rows from L to R.
Select smaller cols to those shown on chart

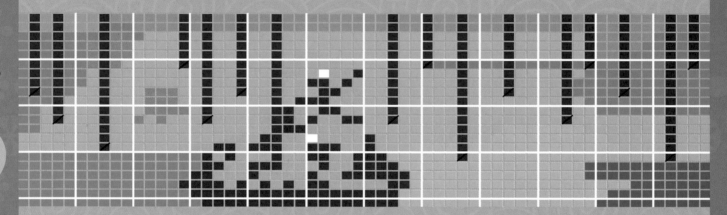

Sts 1 - 57

■ **A**

◪ **Decrease this st by knitting**
together with an adjacent one

Village Green Chart cont. *121 sts x 21 rows*

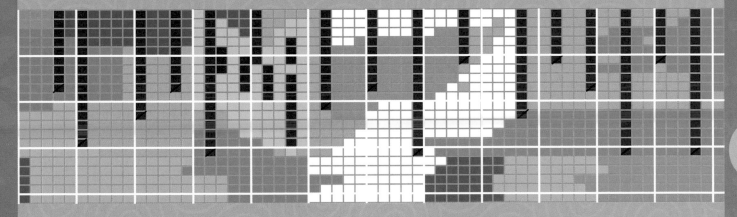

Sts 58-121

This cozy by Teresa Channell features a rural view of intricate detail for aspiring country folk. The pleating technique and dangling sheep motifs make this design really unique.

Rural Vista

Materials

- Double knitting wools approx (175m/191yd per 50g ball)
- 50g in Grass Green (A – split into 2 balls)
- 40g in Sky Blue (B – split into 2 balls)
- 25g in Heather Mix (C – hill split into 4 balls)
- 20g in Fawn (D – wall split into 2 balls)
- 20g in Blue/Green (E – stream split into 2 balls)
- 10g in White (F – cloud and lambs)
- Oddments of embroidery threads or tapestry wool (or mixture)

- Small amounts in Daffodil Yellow (for French knots), Red (poppy rows)
- 3 strands of Green silk for stalk and leaves
- Small square of 7 mesh plastic canvas for lamb
- Size 3.75mm (US5, UK9) needles

Special techniques

- Moss stitch – see page 145
- Pleating – see pattern notes

Pattern notes

Pleats formed by 'yarn pulled behind' for all rows.

Working with 2 or more balls of colour (even when row is all the same colour), ball 1 knit 8 sts, *bring 2nd ball behind back of work and draw it up to ¾in (2cm), k8 using this 2nd ball. Draw first ball across this 2nd block of 8 sts in the same way. Rep from * to end. Twist 2nd ball over 1st ball before starting the next row.

Work cols from back and front chart – omitting colour details (odd yellow and red sts) – these are added later as embroidery.

Cozy

Work 2 pieces alike.

Using 3.75mm needles and A, cast on 96 sts and knit 4 rows (rows 1–4 of chart). Now begin 'yarn pulled behind' for all rows, ie. join in a 2nd ball of green – see patt notes.

Row 35 to end: Change to st st and work in st st throughout using 'thread pulled behind' and working from chart.

Row 60: Begin cloud in sky foll chart (I used moss stitch to add texture).

Row 65: Decrease as shown on chart. When 12 sts rem:

Next row: Work 2tog across the row. Break yarn. Thread through rem 6 sts. Draw up firmly and fasten off.

Making up

Using 2 strands of blue, make a twisted cord 12in (30cm) long. Sew to top of tea cozy to make a 'pull-off loop'. Pull ends through dec sts and add a dangling feature either using lamb chart as a guide to making little lambs, or tassels could be substituted. Using chart and cozy pictures as a guide, embroider 3 yellow French knots for daffodils, red chain sts for tulips and add straight stitches for leaves and stems to tulips using stranded green thread. Join seams (through first and last sts of rows), leaving openings for handle and spout.

Rural Vista Chart *96 sts x 77rows*

Back and Front alike. Front read RS rows from R to L and WS rows L to R, reverse for back.

Each square = 1st and 1 row

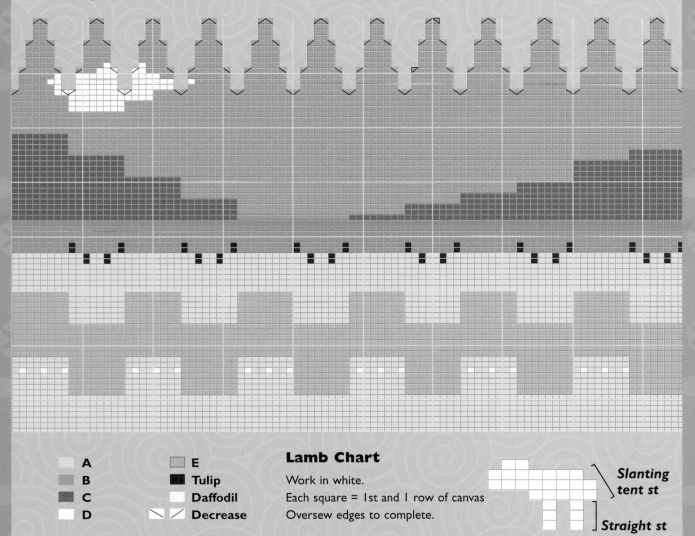

A

B

C

D

E

Tulip

Daffodil

Decrease

Lamb Chart

Work in white.

Each square = 1st and 1 row of canvas

Oversew edges to complete.

Slanting tent st

Straight st

A naked teapot!

Techniques

How to make your prize pot decent

Casting on

1 Form a slip knot on the left-hand needle. Insert the right-hand needle into the loop and wrap the yarn around it as shown.

2 Pull the yarn through the first loop to create a new one.

3 Slide it onto the left-hand needle.

There are now two stitches on the left-hand needle. Continue until you have the desired amount of stitches.

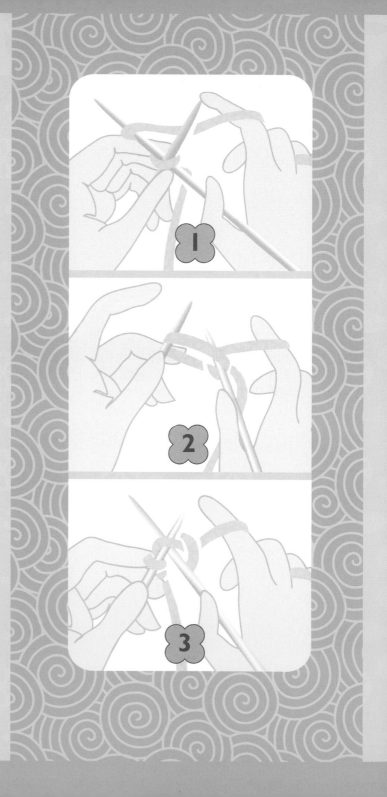

Casting off

1 Knit two stitches onto the right-hand needle, then slip the first stitch over the second and let it drop off the needle. One stitch now remains.

2 Knit another stitch so you have two on the right-hand needle once again. Repeat process until only one stitch is left on the left-hand needle. Break yarn and thread through remaining stitch.

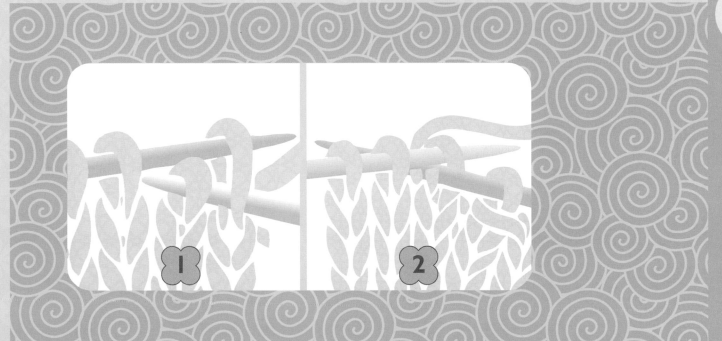

Knit stitch

1 Hold the needle with the cast-on stitches in your left hand. Place the tip of the empty right-hand needle into the first stitch. Wrap the yarn around as for casting on.

2 Pull the yarn through to create a new loop.

3 The new stitch is then slipped onto the right-hand needle.

Continue in the same way for each stitch on the left-hand needle.

To start a new row, swap the needles so that the left needle is full once again and repeat instructions.

Purl stitch

1. The yarn is held to the to the front of the work as shown.

2. Place the right-hand needle into the first stitch from front to back. Wrap the yarn around right-hand needle anticlockwise.

3. Bring the needle back through the stitch and pull through.

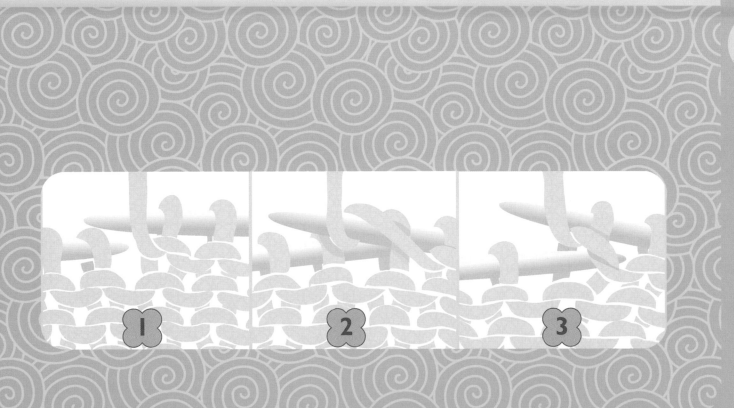

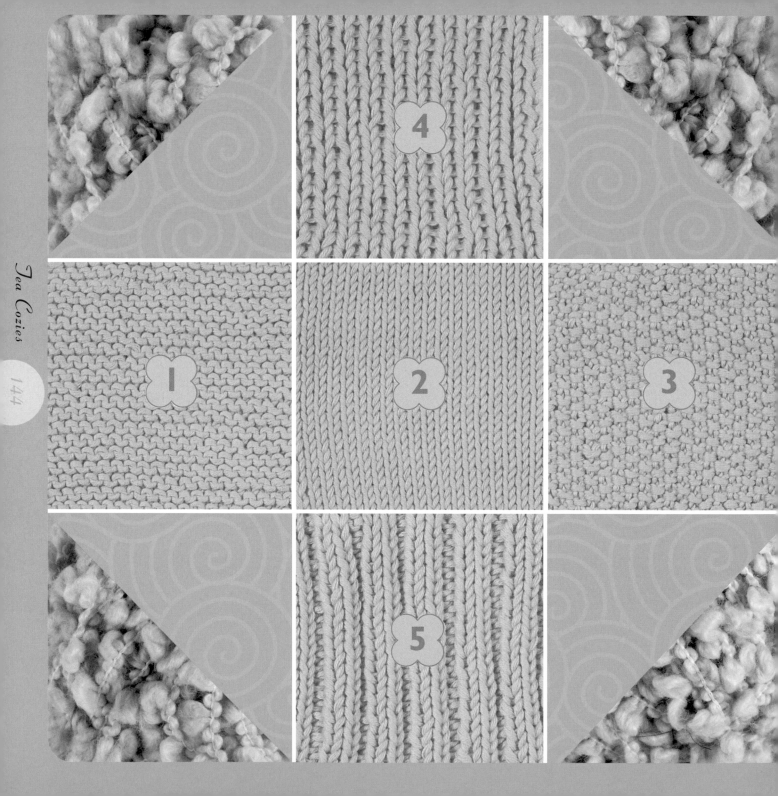

1 Garter stitch

Knit every row.

2 Stocking stitch

Knit on right-side rows and purl
on wrong-side rows.

3 Moss stitch

With an even number of stitches:
Row 1: (K1, P1) to end.
Row 2: (P1, K1) to end.
Repeat rows 1 and 2 to form pattern.
With an odd number of stitches:
Row 1: *K1, P1, rep from * to last st, K1.
Repeat to form pattern.

4 Single rib

With an even number of stitches:
Row 1: *K1, p1* rep to end
Repeat for each row

With an odd number of stitches:
Row 1: *K1, p1, rep from * to last st, k1.
Row 2: *P1, k1, rep from * to last st, p1.

5 Double rib

Row 1: *K2, p2, rep from * to end.
Repeat for each row.

Sewing up

Place the pieces to be joined on a flat surface laid
together side-by-side with right sides towards you. Using
matching yarn, thread a needle back and forth with small,
straight stitches. The stitches form a ladder between the
two pieces of fabric, creating a flat, secure seam.

Other stitches

Loop stitch

K1 without slipping st off L needle. Bring yarn to front (yf) between needles. Wrap yarn around left thumb to form a loop. Bring yarn to back (yb), between the needles, and knit the same stitch again, this time slipping to R needle (2 sts now on R needle). Lift first st over second st and drop it off the needle.

Cable stitch

With the help of a cable needle, these decorative stitches are quite straight forward. Stitches are slipped onto the needle and then knitted later to create the twists.

Cable 4 sts front (4sts cbfr)

1 Slip the next 2 sts onto a cable needle and hold in front of work.

2 Knit the next 2 stitches from the left-hand needle as normal. Then, knit the 2 sts from the cable needle. Cable 4 sts back (4 sts cbbk)

3 Slip the next 2 sts onto a cable needle and hold at back of work.

Knit the next 2 sts from the left-hand needle as normal. Then knit the 2 sts from the cable needle.

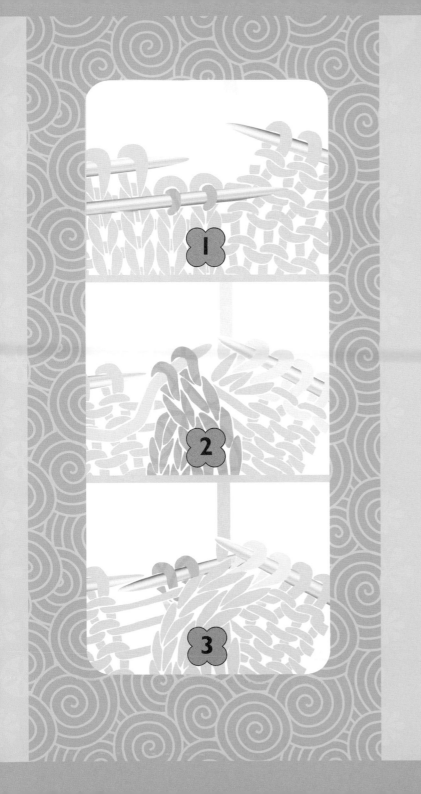

Colour knitting

Intarsia

Blocks of colour are created by using the intarsia technique of twisting the yarns at the back of the work with each colour change (see diagram). It is better to use bobbins than whole balls to prevent tangling. They are smaller and can hang at the back of the work out of the way. Once finished, the ends are weaved in at the back and pressing under a damp cloth will help to neaten any distorted stitches. **1**

Fair isle

Fair Isle knitting uses the stranding technique which involves picking up and dropping yarns as they are needed but unlike intarsia, they are then carried across the row. Loops are formed along the back of the work which should not exceed about 5 stitches in length. Make sure the loops are of even tension otherwise fabric may pucker.

2 Start knitting with the first colour (A) which is dropped when you need to incorporate the second (B). To pick up A again bring under B and knit again.

3 To pick up B again, drop A and bring B over A and knit again.

Crochet

Chain stitch

With hook in right hand and yarn resting over middle finger of left hand, pull yarn taught. Take hook under then over yarn. **1**

Pull the hook and yarn through the loop whilst holding slip knot steady. Repeat action to form a foundation row of chain stitch. **2**

Double crochet

Start by placing hook into a stitch. Wrap new yarn round the hook and draw loop back through work towards you. There should now be two loops on the hook. Yarn around hook once more and then draw through both loops. **3**

There should now be one loop left on the hook.
One double crochet stitch is now complete – repeat to continue row.